MAPS TO ANYWHERE

MAPS TO

ANYWHERE

BERNARD COOPER

THE UNIVERSITY OF GEORGIA PRESS

ATHENS AND LONDON

© 1990 by Bernard Cooper
Published by the University of Georgia Press
Athens, Georgia 30602
All rights reserved
Designed by Louise M. Jones
Set in 10 on 13 Meridien
Printed digitally

Printed in the United States of America

Library of Congress Cataloging-in-Publication Data
Cooper, Bernard, 1951–
Maps to anywhere / Bernard Cooper.
       p.   cm.
ISBN 0-8203-1190-1 (alk. paper)
ISBN 0-8203-1946-5 (pbk. : alk. paper)
I. Title.
AC8 .C654 1990
081—dc20   89-11864

British Library Cataloging-in-Publication Data available

I'm grateful to Jeff Hammond for his many careful readings. I'm also indebted to the following people for their trust, patience, and sound advice: Kerry Burt, John Chase, Jill Ciment, Robert Dawidoff, Tom Knechtel, Dana Gorbea-Leon, Bia Lowe, and Brian Miller.

Special thanks to Richard Howard and Norman Laurila.

Sometimes I breathe harder and all of a sudden, with the aid of my continual absent-mindedness, the world rises and falls with my chest. Perhaps not Africa, but big stuff.

—Henri Michaux

Contents

The End of Manners

The House of the Future

Childless

Foreword

Supple, Tractable, Mutable
A Note on Bernard Cooper

This cluster of texts—a breviary of erotic reconciliation, placating the elegist's theme of loss and longing, in which Cooper's adjectives take the place of Baudelaire's *luxe, calme et volupté* as principles of a lyric art—this *book of songs* begins with nomination ("I wanted to be the man who got to name the paint chips at Bromley's Hardware") and ends in speechlessness ("I walked and walked to hush the world, leaving silence like spoor"). The meditations between, neither fictions nor essays, neither autobiographical illuminations nor cultural inventions but, indeed, something like those paint chips, samples of a domain of user-friendly chromatics, vary greatly in length and intensity; some are prose poems of Baudelairean resource; others are broadsides and spiels which serve as packaging instructions for the products of a highly advanced (self-destructing) consumer culture; all, throughout, suggest a personal history which is *mapped*, as the author so often says, but not *developed*. We are everywhere on the surface of the self-sphere, and not permitted to sink to the metamorphic center, to rise into the heaven of release from identity. No event in this intimate chronicle leads to any other event: nothing *eventuates*, then, but everything recurs, everything celebrates a perpetual efflorescence in Cooper's star-system. That system is indeed, etymologically speaking, a *consideration* of experience in which the Bernard-figure (like the Marcel-figure, neither character nor symbol) devises his responses in constellations, significant *casts of stars*. Again and again, a brother dies, a father remarries, the giant emblems persevere like dinosaurs in the primeval landscape, and we may not see them from that normalizing perspective by which we know we are grown up; there is in fact no adult view in *Maps to Anywhere,* for that implication would be one of terminus and judgment. And in the strangely *indulged* world of these texts, there is no conclusion, merely recurrence; no verdict, merely wonder. *Merely!* It is Cooper's very achievement to have suspended such maturities, to have inveigled us so readily into an immediately recognizable American Eden, the whereabouts of the mobile home . . .

Movies and radio, television and malls—these constitute the culture which affords the imagery Cooper deploys; no theater, no art, no music to sweeten the spirit's functions. And being Jewish—in Los Angeles, at least—is no help at all; where, one may ask, are the people of the Book? No, the camera and the internal-combustion engine are the alpha and omega of this world; all that was once so inveterately scribal and tribal (in Malamud, in both Roths) has been elided. Not only the parents, but the sons as well are dinosaurs:

> There are guys at my gym whose latissimus dorsi, having spread like thunderheads, cause them to inch through an ordinary door; might the dinosauria have grown too big of their own volition? . . . Once, I imagined our exercise through X-ray eyes. Our skeletons gaped at their own reflection. Empty eyes, like apertures, opened onto an afterlife. Lightning-bright spines flashed from sacrums. Phalanges of hands were splayed in surprise. Bones were glowing everywhere. . . . And I knew our remains were meant to keep like secrets under the earth. And I knew one day we would topple like monuments, stirring up clouds of dust. And I almost heard the dirge of our perishing, thud after thud after thud, our last titanic exhalations loud and labored and low.

Certainly this is prose of a very high order, or even of a very high chaos, but what captivates me about it, what attaches me to it in this prefatory way (for Cooper "needs" no introduction: he is as accessible as Disneyland, as alluring as the La Brea tar pits) is the odd autonomy of its invention: not derived from vestiges of culture like Sontag and Barthelme, not framed by visions of excess like Elkin and McElroy, here is a self-begotten American dialect which composes, with great modesty and sweetness, what Barthes calls *the text of pleasure;* here comedy, however rueful, is never a *shtick,* here the sense of personal inadequacy, however hilarious, is never guilty or hysterical. Most writers, even the American exemplars I have named, regard the body as, at some level, on some principle, an enemy; it is Cooper's distinction, his rare and pervasive entertainment of somatic sympathies—what I like to call his polymorphous propriety—which makes him, as Herbert once said, so fresh, new and quick.

Richard Howard

Acknowledgments

Portions of this book have appeared in the following reviews:

The Georgia Review: "Beacons Burning Down" and "How to Draw"

Grand Street: "Maps to Anywhere," "Sudden Extinction," "Utopia," and "The House of the Future"

The Indiana Review: "Childless"

The Louisville Review: "The End of Manners"

The Michigan Quarterly Review: "Atlantis"

The Malahat Review: "Temple of the Holy Ghost," "Gravitational Attraction," "The Theory of Relativity," and "Ark"

Mississippi Mud: "The Biggest, Most Beautiful Balcony in the World"

The Ohio Journal: "Leaving," "Spontaneous Combustion"

The Santa Monica Review: "Saturday Night"

The Seattle Review: "Duet"

Shenandoah: "Auld Lang Syne," "Capiche?," "The Hurricane Ride," "Make It Good," "On the Air," "The Origins of Roget's Thesaurus," and "Potato Spirit"

The Southeast Review: "Futurism"

Sun Dog–The Southeast Review: "Futurism"

The Western Humanities Review: "Live Wire," "Aphorism," "Rain Rambling Through Japan," "Don't Think About Breathing," and "The Wind Did It"

"Beacons Burning Down" was reprinted in *The Best American Essays of 1988,* edited by Annie Dillard.

"By Any Other Name," a section from "Beacons Burning Down," was reprinted in *Life Studies: A Thematic Reader* (St. Martin's Press).

"Dream House," a section from "The House of the Future," was reprinted in *Harper's*.

"Sudden Extinction" was reprinted in *The Art of Science Writing* (Teachers and Writers Collaborative).

Several of these pieces appeared in a limited-edition chapbook titled *On the Air* (Abattoir Editions, University of Nebraska at Omaha, 1989).

MAPS TO ANYWHERE

BEACONS
BURNING DOWN

By Any Other Name

"Mr. Felix Ott?"

"Yes, this is Felix."

"Greetings! This is the (mumble, mumble) radio program calling. If you can answer today's quiz question correctly, you will be the winner of a two-hundred-dollar cash prize."

"How many hundred?"

"Now listen closely: If Elvis Presley's nickname is Elvis the Pelvis, Mr. Ott, what—for the cash—is the nickname of his brother, Enis?"

A long pause in which our hearts were pounding and our breath held back, and then we would start to sputter and laugh, three kids with flushed faces crowded around the earpiece of the phone. Not one of our intended victims was fool enough to venture a guess, not Birdie Turley, Gilliam Ong, Venus Deitz, Lafayette Lipshitz, Panos Injijikian, Porntip Yang, or Buster Hummer, names we picked from the phone book after great deliberation, after gales of hysteria which left us limp on the sea-green carpet. We'd base our choice on assonance, or on the alliteration some parents had bestowed, a mellifluous gift to their offspring which made us roll our eyes. More poets than pranksters, we thrilled to language in its abstract conditions, were amazed by the ways a name could bluster and make us as giddy as the pop tunes of the time: *My boy lollipop, he makes my heart go giddy-up* and *Da do ron ron ron, da do ron ron.*

But our most significant discoveries, extracted from alphabetical columns, were the names in which a sentence was encoded: Iva Wright, Hugo First, Pat A. Head, R. U. Standing. To find them took hours of textual analysis, and often, after much vetoing and page turning, we were so embroiled in the nonsense of sound (our minds balked, our eyes blurred) that it was hard to tell if those flukes of unintended syntax were the genuine article or the product of imagination. Were we trying to will meaning into being? Jeffrey, the youngest among us, would become nearly delirious from our endeavor. Entranced by any old ordinary word, he'd begin to say it over and over. Mary, his sister, once let out an ear-splitting scream because, after a flurry of crank calls, Jeffrey sat in a corner incessantly chanting "cheese."

It would be five years before I heard Shakespeare's comment on the name for a rose, but had I heard it then, I'm afraid I'd have disagreed. For example, wasn't the smell of Limburger somehow linked to its foul sound? Weren't the forget-me-nots blooming on Mary's blouse made softer and bluer by their designation? Weren't names designed to enhance the matter to which they referred?

My own name was problematic. While Jeff and Mary could go to the five-and-dime and find cups and wallets bearing their names—evidence that they belonged to a vast and accepted subset of humanity—Bernard was always out of the question, however much I'd spin the racks and dig in the bins with hope: Andy, Art, Bill, Bobby, Charles. Even my mother had trouble with my name; calling me home at dusk, she'd stand in the doorway and shout the names of my older brothers—Richard, Robert, Ronald!—before she remembered mine. A recurring dream I have involves just this childhood scene, but in the dream my mother keeps bellowing names, and soon her friends and relatives, the postman and the grocer, her hairdresser and her podiatrist—*everyone*—converges on the house, her voice drawing life from the dream's dark corners.

In an attempt to make up for her habitual oversight, my mother once showed me the page in *What to Name the Baby* that explained the derivation of Bernard. Far from the bearish obstinance and earthiness the name was said to imply, it held for me the connotations of myopia, introversion, and bookishness that my destiny has borne out. But more important, I was astonished that the mothers of America were so unmoved by their own sense of cadence that they had to rely on a book. In those days I had little inclination toward being a parent, yet I imagined play-ing with my progeny and wondered what I'd call them. Soon I came up with Praline for a girl (this came to me one night during dessert), and Conch for a boy (a visit to Marineland). Perhaps it was the common ring of my brothers' names that led them to dub their daughters Dalisa, Cambria, and Jordana, names as strange as orchids at the florist's—throats on fire with purple and pink as though they're about to announce what they are: Cymbidium, Miltonia, Cattleya.

Running the gamut from airplane pilot to zoologist, the am-bitions of my playmates were subject to daily fluctuations. For almost a year I wanted to be the man who got to name the paint chips at Bromley's Hardware. I'd cram them in my pockets, sneak them home, fan them open, contemplate. Fiesta Magenta, Magma Red, Sunstroke, Topaz, Obsidian, Smoke. Surely the advent of metallic and fluorescent paint would increase the de-mand for persons with my calling. I pictured myself with a huge palette, mixing new additions to the language of chromatics. Before me loomed a long good life—Carrot Orange, Eden Green —of indulgence in the spectrum.

Unfortunately, my schoolwork suffered as a result of my pas-sion for nomenclature. In biology, for instance, instead of con-centrating on the position and function of the bones in the skeletal system, I imagined Ulna, Tibia, and Fibula as visitors from outer space; during lengthy fantasies I'd try to teach them English. Astronomy, on the other hand, with its vocabulary of umbra, penumbra, corona, and nova, was inspiration for the names of colors, but shed little light on my place among the planets. Reading was the only subject at which I excelled—espe-cially poetry, a treasure-trove of rhyme from which one melo-dramatic teacher, her arms akimbo, her glasses awry, would unearth a jewel like "Gitchie Gumee."

One trick I learned in the sixth grade (and which tempts me to this day) was to yell out the names of passengers while traveling through a tunnel. There was something elegiac in hearing the

names of friends I loved—Mary *ary ary*, Jeff *eff eff*—rebounding
against the underground walls, buffeted by oncoming traffic,
fading with every echo. And then we'd be restored to the light
and the road, and the sky was robin's egg blue, and a cringing
parent behind the wheel would admonish me by name, two
syllables rippling out on the surface of time.

The Heralds

Religion meant people with shrouded heads mumbling
in gaudy, vaulted chambers. I sank when I saw a deacon's censer
wafting incense into the world like the tailpipe of a hot rod. Or
rabbis who davened like wind-up toys. Or meditating Buddhist
monks as stock still as my rock collection. Once, *Life* magazine featured "The Great Cathedrals of Europe," and what I
saw, or tasted rather, after turning the pages and licking my
index finger, was the bitterness of ink, a flavor that matched the
photographs of expressionless death masks, prostrate statues,
apothecary jars (more ornate than our pharmacist's) in which
slept slivers of the saints.

You don't really expect me to believe that Joseph Smith translated the Book of Mormon by picking up a gold Roman soldier's
breastplate he found in the forest and peering through the holes
where the nipples would have been, do you? Think about it.
Either Mr. Smith's eyes would have to be very far apart, or the
soldier who fortuitously left his armor had a chest cavity the
size of the average cranium. I mean, I wish it were true. I wish
I could find it and spend the afternoon reading translations of
the "Inferno" and the "Kama Sutra" through a beautiful amber
mask. But I was exempted from miracles way back in kinder-
garten when I watched *Romper Room* on television, and the
hostess, Miss Mary, with her high, sibylline voice, would give
a long look into the camera and claim to see right through
the cathode tube to her flock of amazed and devoted children.
"There's Judy," she'd intone, or "I spy David and Suzy and

Frank." But it never occurred to her that there was a child out there with a name as strange as "Bernard," so I knew she was a charlatan.

Look, I like cherubim as much as the next guy. They've got good intentions and tiny genitalia. They must smell and feel like lilac sachets. My life, however, is busy and baroque without their intervention. Sure, I've got work enough for a legion of angels: insurmountable personal fears, a vendetta against international evil, friends to raise from the dead. Why, just yesterday I was lamenting all these things when I saw a stream of black birds soaring over the city. Endless they were, like winged pieces of letters, like a moving sign in Times Square, heraldic and quick and colossal. Except that a message never appeared. Their transmigration riddled the sky.

The Miracle Chicken
(Glimpses into My Father's Scrapbook)

On March 30, 1940, the day he was notified that he had passed the California state bar examination, my father began a scrapbook with two items: a letter requesting a seven-dollar fee that entitled him to become a legitimate attorney and a solicitation from a wholesaler of leather-bound law books. After that come a hundred buckled newspaper clippings that betray his taste for handling unorthodox cases.

One article is emblazoned with the headline "CASE OF THE BAKING NEWLYWED," about Mrs. Beverly Cleveland, a woman who claimed her husband Jake kept her cooking from dawn to dusk during the first ten days of marriage—waffles, casseroles, pies from scratch—so that no time was left for affection. But my father subpoenaed witnesses who testified under oath that Jake Cleveland's appetite was notoriously meager. "Never ate what *I* slaved to make," whispered his first wife under her breath. "Just look at the guy—he's built like a broom," said Mr. Luft of the *Chow Now* lunch truck. In his final argument, my father spoke of his "kissless client" whose "connubial crisis" was exacerbated during a ten-day "hellmoon." Not only was there an annulment, but my father convinced the court to fine the former Mrs. Cleveland fifty dollars in punitive damages for wasting groceries in a ploy to avoid her wifely obligation.

Profiting from the frequency of tumultuous marriages, my father moved his office into wood-paneled quarters on the fifth floor of the elegant Biscott Building. On his door was stenciled "Edward S. Cooper" in large gold letters. "Attorney at Law" was relegated to a smaller, less illustrious print. On the sill behind his desk, he placed a brass statuette of justice: her toga cleaved her figure as though she were walking against the wind; her scales, loaded with candy, bobbed in the slightest breeze.

The office windows overlooked a small park frequented at noon by secretaries—Caucasian, Asian, Hispanic, black—wearing cat-eye glasses held in place by chains. Some of them met my father for assignations over the years in a dark downtown hotel. His lust for the opposite sex (in all their ethnic variety), his clandestine romances, his cultivation of a subterfuge my mother didn't suspect until she was in her sixties—these made him all the more adept at drumming up the deceits that made his divorce trials so bathetic they became genuinely sad, reminding everyone who followed them in the papers that, when love sought justice, both were blind.

And yet my father's most publicized trial had nothing to do with the vicissitudes of human love, though the case of the Miracle Chicken would outstrip his previous arbitrations with its sheer theatricality, media appeal, and metaphysical intimations. Filed in superior court on April 20, 1950, Mrs. Martha Green's suit against the Society for the Prevention of Cruelty to Animals describes how she purchased a three-and-one-half-pound rooster, with its head cut off, at a San Bernardino market. She placed it in the bottom of her grocery bag and covered it with at least ten pounds of "victuals." Six hours later she lifted oranges, potatoes, and eggs from the bag, and up fluttered the headless rooster. For four days Mrs. Green reverently nurtured her miracle, naming him Lazarus and feeding him a solution of raw egg and warm milk through an eyedropper. Hundreds of people ventured to her home to glimpse the creature. It was even rumored that a famous actress asked to feed the bird personally, squeezing the vital drops with bejeweled fingers as her chauffeur held its wings. Many people prayed at the sight of Lazarus, some claiming to be instantaneously cured of lifelong afflictions, including one woman who flung away her crutches with the remark, "If that bird can get along without a head, I can get along without these crutches."

Then two men from the city humane department intruded with an order that Mrs. Green either put the chicken out of its misery within twelve hours or face imprisonment. Instead, early that night, under cover of darkness, Mrs. Green smuggled Lazarus to a local veterinarian, Dr. Allan Rice, rather than kill him a second time. But Dr. Rice hardly had time to make Lazarus comfortable (in a cage lined with newspapers full of reports about Mrs. Green) before the two SPCA men came and forcibly took the bird—deaf and blind to this onslaught of intrigue—to an undisclosed location.

At midnight, in a frenzy of apprehension, Mrs. Green had a vision in which a benevolent, faceless figure in a feathered cloak walked into her bedroom through the southeast wall and implored her to consider chapter 9, verse 8 in the Gospel According to Saint Matthew: "When the multitude saw it they marveled and glorified God which had given power unto men." That's when she phoned my father.

Photographed beside the brooding Mrs. Green, my father tried to address the issue from a perspective both secular and devout, telling the reporter from *Life* magazine that Lazarus had come to Mrs. Green as an act of providence for the interest and benefit of science and mankind—adding that she wanted him back, or five thousand bucks. Meanwhile, Father hired a filmmaker to document the incident for posterity, and the scrapbook contains an itemization of the man's expenditures, including pancake makeup for Mrs. Green, extra eggs for Lazarus, gas to San Bernardino and back. But perhaps the most worthwhile expenditure was for the poster that advertised the film. This was inset with snapshots of a lump with wings, a question mark hovering over its head, the layout rampant with boldface captions: THE MIRACLE CHICKEN. NOT A HOLLYWOOD MAKE-BELIEVE MOVIE. HEADLESS ROOSTER HOPE OF MILLIONS. BIRD CURES BLIND, LAME AND SICK. HUMBLE HOME OF MYSTIC BIRD A SHRINE.

The public sentiment in favor of Mrs. Green prompted the SPCA to forgo a court battle and return Lazarus only one week after his abduction, with a decorous apology broadcast on radio. Accompanied by the two henchmen, the miracle was wrapped in a blue flannel blanket. After being examined by Dr. Rice, Lazarus was handed over to the beaming Mrs. Green, her eyedropper at the ready.

Little was said when Lazarus died quietly a few months later. Only my father came to pay condolences, as sure as Mrs. Green that the hoopla had killed it, that no one on earth can cope with divinity. While Mrs. Green lowered the large coffee can containing Lazarus into his grave, my father doffed his fedora and shielded his eyes against the sun.

For years after, he collected every reference to the precedent of the Miracle Chicken. The last page of his scrapbook is covered by a column entitled "Blames Bubble in Mercy Case," in which a physician is accused of injecting an air bubble into the comatose Mrs. Abbie C. Borroto, thus causing a fatal embolism. During his cross-examination Dr. Robert Biron, an expert witness, was grilled by the attorney for the prosecution regarding the clinical definition of death:

"Dr. Biron, have you ever seen a chicken with its head cut off?"

"Yes."

"If a chicken's head is cut off, and the body is still moving, is the chicken dead or alive?"

"There is life in the tissue."

"Just tell me, Dr. Biron, is that chicken still living?"

"I can't answer that. There is life in the tissue."

"I repeat, Doctor, is a chicken with his head cut off still living? Just answer yes or no."

"I can't answer that. That is impossible to answer."

. . . .

Eighty-one years old, retired, my father is just out of the hospital after an operation to drain a pool of water that had formed around his heart. Gaining weight again, he eats lunch with gusto, telling me about echocardiograms as he looks into the mirrored walls of the Crystal Room, his haunt, and catches a glimpse of himself, alive and almost infinite. Then he shifts his gaze to the silver-haired waitress who, all busy reflection, seems to scatter in different directions like a drop of mercury. Assuming that I too find her alluring, he looks at me and cocks an eyebrow.

All afternoon, conversation fluctuates between his brush with death—cold kiss of the stethoscope, bitter breathfuls of ether—and a running commentary on the waitress, responding now to his winks and piling our empty plates on her arm, her freckled cleavage seeming to stir in him an impulse as strong as the will to survive. His eyes grow moist at the advent of arousal, each brown iris blazing with highlights. When he pivots to track that aproned anatomy, I can see from across the table that his head of white hair, redolent of tonic, is faintly yellow like old pages.

I hand him back his scrapbook before I hug him good-bye, and I hug him good-bye with a fierceness that startles even me. His iridescent suit, within my embrace, displays its shades of dark and light. I tell him I'm just trying to wring the last of the water out of him. It's a miracle, I tell him, that the heart can float.

Chapter After Chapter

When the symbolist poets spoke of "Le Livre," the voluminous book into which all experience settles as beautiful language, it is improbable, but not impossible, that they had someone like my mother in mind. Weekly, she'd announce another anecdote, wrenched from her past, that she planned to immortalize in the book of her life, the tome she absolutely without fail was going to write just as soon as she was less busy and had some extra cash. But the longer the book was postponed, and the farther away she was from the original events, the less truthful these stories became. Preposterously exaggerated, they were told with eerie, quivering conviction.

My favorite was about how she swam to America from Russia. She was two, she said. The dark, salty ocean was quite an adversary, but her parents were of strong stock and excellent swimmers.

How could I have believed her? Why did I carry with me, all through my childhood, an image of Mother, Grandma and Grandpa, arising fully clothed like phantoms from the breakers, stopping for a moment to pant on the sand, then proceeding, hands linked, hems wet and limp, into a new society?

On the other hand, were my mother alive today, she would probably doubt the importance of the anecdotes I reserve for paper.

For example, yesterday, driving to a play, I sat in my car, stalled in traffic, and watched a slow cavalcade of honking cars. It was a wedding of the type I'd forgotten—streamer-laden American cars, perfectly polished, their antennas crowned with balloons and bouquets. Bride and groom led the procession, blushing and beaming with hope. Brimming carloads of friends followed, their faces charged with vicarious bliss. Then the parents, their smiles weary, their car like an ominous cloud. After that, a few cars of total strangers honked sarcastically just for the fun of it. Finally the onrushing rest of the world, late for their lives, their wives and routines. Horns cried and foreheads sweated. I seemed to feel their awful impatience as I cautiously turned and edged in among them. It was 5:35, late in August. Sun filled the windshield.

I was late for the play. It was very bad. The protagonist, a fallen man, drank and confessed, drank and confessed, stumbling toward an epiphany. The set was dim and he stared into air, screaming to his departed mother, "Your eyes are like beacons burning down!" As the lights came up, I blushed with embarrassment, believing both art and life were hopeless.

Yet hours later that line began to haunt me, move me by virtue of its obvious corniness. And by midnight I grew to love that line, the way you come to love an intimate's obvious weakness. I tossed and turned in a kind of wild rapture, trying to find a way to write my mother's book for her, and I'm sorry to say I can't, I'd like to, but I'm just too busy writing my own book, or trying to, and it's really difficult. But if I could, the dust jacket would be beautiful, and in between would be long, eloquent, haunting passages about the big tumultuous ocean, and the sun in August, and life in the city, and the dedication would make you cry, and I'd title it *Beacons Burning Down*.

··

ATLANTIS

Atlantis

How did the barber pole originate? When did its characteristic stripes become kinetic, turning hypnotically, driven by a hidden motor, giving the impression of red and blue forever twining, never slowing? No matter. No icon or emblem, no symbol or sign, still or revolving, lit from within or lit from without, could in any way have prepared me for that haircut at Nick's Barber Shop, or for Nick himself. His thick Filipino accent obscured meaning, though the sound was mellifluous, and the sense, translated in the late afternoon light, was expressed in the movements of Nick's hands. He flourished a comb he never dropped, a soundless scissors, a razor which revealed, gently, gently, the nape of my neck, now so smooth, attuned to the wind and the wool of my collar.

After our initial exchange of misunderstood courtesies, Nick nudged me toward a wall, museum bright, on which hung a poster depicting the "Official Haircuts for Men and Boys" from 1955. I understood immediately that I was to choose from among the Brush Cut, the Ivy League, the Flat Top with Fenders. To insure sanctity and a sense of privacy, Nick turned off the fan for a moment, lowered his head, and even the dust stopped drifting in abeyance. Above me, in every phase from profile to full front, were heads of hair, luxuriant, graphic, lacquer-black: outmoded curls like scrolls on entablature, sideburns rooted in the past, strands and locks in arrested motion, cresting waves styled into hard edges, like Japanese prints of typhoons.

None of the heads contained a face. One simply interjected his own face. These oval vessels waited to be filled again and again by men's imaginations. For decades, they absorbed the eyes and noses and lips of customers who stood on the checkerboard of old linoleum, or sat in salmon-pink chairs next to wobbling tables stacked with magazines featuring bikinis and ballgames. The haircut was over in no time. (Nick did a stint in the army, where expedience is everything.) I kept my eyes closed. But aware of strange and lovely afterimages—ghostly pay phone, glowing push broom—I seemed to be submerged in the rapture of the deep. The drone of the fan, the minty and intoxicating scent of Barbasol pressed upon me; phosphene shimmered like minnows in the dark corners of my vision, and I found that this world, cigar stained, sergeant striped, basso profundo, was the lost world of my father, who could not love me. So when Nick kneaded my shoulders and pressed my temples (free scalp manipulation with every visit), I unconsciously grazed him like a cat in Atlantis. His fingers flowed over my forehead like water. I began to smile imperceptibly and see barber poles aslant like sunken columns and voluptuous mermaids in salmon-pink bikinis and bubbles the size of baseballs rising to the surface and bursting with snippets of Filipino small talk.

I can't tell you how odd it was when, restored by a splash of astringent tonic, I finally opened my eyes and saw a clump of my own hair, blown by the fan, skitter across the floor like a cat. For a moment the mirrors were unbearably silver, and the hand-lettered signs, reflected in reverse, seemed inscriptions in a long-forgotten language.

Indeed I looked better, contented. Older too in the ruddy light of sunset. And all of this, this seminal descent to the floor of the sea, this inundation of two paternal hands, this sudden maturation in the mirror, for only four dollars and fifty cents. But my debt of gratitude, beyond the dollar-fifty tip, will be paid here, in the form of Nick's actual telephone number, area code (213) 660-4876. Even his business card, adorned with a faceless haircut holding a phone, says, "Call any time!" Nick means any time. He means day or night. I've driven by and glimpsed him asleep in the barber chair, his face turned toward the street, his combs soaking in blue medicinal liquid, the barber pole softly aglow like a nightlight, the stripes cascading endlessly down, rivulets running toward a home in the ocean.

Capiche?

In Italy, the dogs say bow-bow instead of bow-wow, and my Italian teacher, Signora Marra, is not quite sure why this should be. When we tell her that here in America the roosters say cock-a-doodle-do, she throws back her head like a hen drinking raindrops and laughs uncontrollably, as if we were fools to believe what our native red rooster says, or ignoramuses not to know that Italian roosters scratch and preen and clear their gullets before reciting Dante to the sun.

In Venice there is a conspicuous absence of dogs and roosters, but all the pigeons on the planet seem to roost there, and their conversations are deafening. When the city finally sinks, only a thick dark cloud of birds will be left to undulate over the ocean, birds kept alive by pure nostalgia and a longing to land. And circulating among them will be stories, reminiscences, anecdotes of all kinds to help pass the interminable days. Even when this voluble cloud dissipates, the old exhausted birds drowning in the sea, the young bereft birds flying away, the sublime and untranslatable tale of the City of Canals will echo off the oily water, the walls of vapor, the nimbus clouds.

There were so many birds in front of Café Florian's, and mosquitoes sang a piercing song as I drank my glass of red wine. Waving them away, I inadvertently beckoned Sandro, a total stranger. With great determination, anxious to know me, he bounded around tables of tourists.

The Piazza San Marco holds many noises within its light-bathed walls, sounds that clash, are superimposed or densely layered like torte. Within that cacophony of words and violins, Sandro and I struggled to communicate. Something unspoken suffered between us. We were, I think, instantly in love, and when he offered me, with his hard brown arms, a blown glass ashtray shaped like a gondola, all I could say, all I could recall of Signora Marra's incanting and chanting (she believed in saturating students in rhyme), was "No capiche." I tried to inflect into that phrase every modulation of meaning, the way different tonalities of light had changed the meaning of that city.

But suddenly this adventure is over. Everything I have told you is a lie. Almost everything. There is no lithe and handsome Sandro. I've never learned Italian or been to Venice. Signora Marra is a feisty fiction. But lies are filled with modulations of untranslatable truth, and early this morning when I awoke, birds were restless in the olive trees. Dogs tramped through the grass and growled. The local rooster crowed fluently. The Chianti sun was coming up, intoxicating, and I was so moved by the strange, abstract trajectories of sound that I wanted to take you with me somewhere, somewhere old and beautiful, and I honestly wanted to offer you something, something like the prospect of sudden love, or color postcards of chaotic piazzas, and I wanted you to listen to me as if you were hearing a rare recording by Enrico Caruso. All I had was the glass of language to blow into a souvenir.

The Biggest, Most Beautiful Balcony in the World

I used to play a game I'd invented with my niece. It had no name, or maybe we called it "What's in the World," or maybe that was what I named it, years later, in memory. Its premise was simple. In rapid succession, I'd ask her what was the saddest thing in the world, or the ugliest, funniest, loudest. And although I can't recall, for the sake of either sentiment or posterity, even one of her answers, I can tell you how the game strained her concentration, and how, sitting perfectly still, she managed, as though leaving her body, to scour the world for an answer. I mean "world" in the elemental sense—shapely continents as suggestive as clouds; the bulging graph of latitude and longitude resting starkly on oceans; the Himalayas, Alps, and other chilly, exhilarating altitudes.

My niece outgrew the game in no time. Now she stays well within the bounds of her body. Now she wants a big house and a handsome husband, and she shall have them.

But yesterday I saw the saddest balcony in the world, a lone balcony jutting out from a stucco apartment building. It overlooked an alley and parking lot, the pavement potholed, lumpy and littered, flanked by trash bins painted a flaking industrial green and caution orange, like large abandoned barges. People wandered through the lot, argued, kissed, talked, and gestured unabashedly among themselves, as if only the immediate mattered: a sharp word or a hungry wink.

It wasn't simply the idea of actually dwelling above this dismal view that made the balcony sad. The thick declining light contributed, and also the shabby curtains drawn behind the sliding glass doors, a leitmotif of misery in this temporal city. The little hibachi didn't help, cheerlessly implying that someone could be sated on that strip over fumes and intrigue. The diamond patterns in the thin gray railing were utterly ironic. Perhaps it was a constellation of all these effects, a suffusion of decay and summer melancholy.

I wanted another, better life, and another bigger, more ornate balcony to gaze up at, something rococo in the brisk abiding sky of northern Europe, an otherworldly ornament hovering in thin air, befitting Juliet Capulet maybe, so timid and exquisite, or a knowing, nodding pope in purple, or any one of several major politicians, squeezing a wife, faithfully waving, and I would stand beneath them all, perfectly happy, no, ecstatic, rapt, eager to profess my affection, and accept my forgiveness, finally, finally, and applaud the sunlit symbol of a new regime.

Potato Spirit

All week long, my mind has been filled with baked potatoes, aluminum-covered ingots, their plumes of steam obscuring everything, except my affection for friends.

If I were to paint portraits of my friends, each would be posed before a fresh hot potato, condensation softening their features, beading chins with a faint opalescence, bringing color to cheeks. See the wrinkled foil refract, filling the air with light. Even my unfortunate friend is intent, staring into a white fissure, watching crystals of salt dissolve, his sadness dispelled by a gust of fragrant vapor.

Potatoes have the burden of a bad reputation: dirty and mealy and starchy, drudgery for teeth and tongue. Van Gogh's painting *The Potato Eaters* has been especially detrimental, giving the consumption of potatoes an irreparable aura of dankness—the peasants' eyes weary with premonitions, the room as dark as a bad dream, a repast of pale, impasto blobs which could never appease the growl of human hunger.

Now let me show you another painting, also entitled *The Potato Eaters,* which I hope will help counteract the infamy of potatoes. In it, my parents struggle with Lester and Cora, their two best friends. Eight elbows and arms lead the viewers' attention to the apex of turmoil. There, in the air, at the ends of all their fingers, one can read, correctly accounted, the cumulative cost of four baked potatoes scrawled on a coffee shop check. To pay this bill would be privilege itself, as basic and pure as potatoes. (Note that these potato skins are rendered in a tender brown, each lying open like a satisfying book.)

Open volume 18 of the *Encyclopedia Britannica.* After Poetry and before Prose, there is an extensive section on Potatoes. It leaves the reader informed about the inarguable importance of world potato production. Tables and graphs lend credence to a new definition of our planet as so much ancient acreage ceaselessly yielding potatoes. Earth is a mine of minerals manifest in each plump tuber. There is even mention of a race in which the winner is he or she who embraces the greatest heap of potatoes and bears them triumphantly to the end. And unbelievably, there is something called Potato Spirit. It is not what I at first thought, really hoped, it would be—a preternatural sensitivity to potatoes, an *Esprit de Potato* as the French might express it, or for the Germans, *Potatogeist*. Rather, it is the absolute essence of *Solanum tuberosum,* the potent liquor of pressed potato, distilled into a faceted glass, raised to propose this toast:

> May portraits of family be unveiled.
> May pages be read and facts digested.
> May your hungry friends be fed.

Rain Rambling
Through Japan

Midway through the semester, a girl in Miss Thompson's composition class dyes her hair black, changes her name to Zephyr, and fills her essays with invented words. Sun "yarbles" through the curtains. The government is shamelessly "euté."
Miss Thompson dares her to use "depooled" in a sentence. Zephyr does.
Miss Thompson's cheeks begin to tingle. "Dear," she says, "those are neologisms. Language, you see, is a consistent system of sounds and symbols . . ."
"All right," snaps Zephyr. "Don't make a brouhaha."

It has been discovered that the Japanese hear the sounds of nature with the hemisphere of the brain usually reserved for the processing of language, so that the suction of mud in the paddies or the ubiquitous hiss of the rain contain a syntactical message. That night, in Miss Thompson's dream, she tries to explain this to a class of black-haired students with names like Jiro Kitagawa and Yuki Noguchi. The rustling of pages in English-to-Japanese dictionaries sounds like a sudden downpour. Lightning punctuates the dream scene, and over and over, thunder pronounces its name.
Outside, in the storm, is Tokyo. The whole population seems to have stopped, heads cocked, patient as ravens, intent as on a brilliant conversation.
"Wish you were here to listen to the rain." Miss Thompson writes this on a blank postcard, though she cannot picture the receiver's face, can't settle on terms to describe how rain

is words, important words rambling through Japan, tangents rapidly running down gutters, adverbs darkening asphalt, adjectives beading the leaves.

Miss Thompson awakes to what she thinks is rain. It's the dream emitting the last of its static. Another school day, bright and warm. And the world, depooled, withholds its wisdom.

On the Air

Why is it that, when people envision the city of the future, they picture domed buildings as buoyant as bubbles, roadways like ribbons unfurling in air, skyscrapers piercing the clouds? It's as if the past were sinking like lead, while the feather-light future defies gravity.

Louis Boullet, living in France in the 1700s, was the foremost utopian planner of his time. The roof of his famous cenotaph was round, a glorious, self-sufficient planet. But Boullet drank, hated his wife, envied the elite who hired him. Besides, heavy with historical references, his buildings never truly soared.

I prefer the futuristic cities in comic strips, odd and purposeless cities: a labyrinthine city stretching underground, a shrunken city in a tyrant's ring, an invisible city you don't know you're visiting, and especially cities afloat like giant clouds.

Think of looking down on the unencumbered earth from a slowly flying city. The shadow of your house is as big as a lake over furrowed fields of wheat. Your portal swings open to the stratosphere. If you could drop leaflets, what would they say?

I'd drop the story of Herbert Morris, radio reporter, who covered the fatal landing of the Hindenburg, Lakehurst, New Jersey, 1937. I'd write how I was busy painting his portrait, a homage in heightened color. I'd write how his passionate voice gave me chills. He said, "Disaster," and his voice was shattered. He said, "Oh, no. Please, please," and you knew he wanted to stop time, to urge the fireball into reverse, like a crimson flower folding up at dusk. He would have if he could have. And most important, I'd tell how he was fired for crying on the air.

In the portrait, his teardrops are darkly outlined. You can't just turn away from them. They can't be dismissed as mere abstractions. They really well up. They really burn.

Meanwhile, aboard the flying city (which has nothing to do with the malls, condominiums, or megastructures of the present), my dream house is gliding over dolphin-dotted seas. I will finish the portrait and print my leaflets by the time we reach the next continent. Already the city into which I was born, with its towers and tenements, trestles and gutters, with its people who live their long lives as witnesses, is sinking like lead below the brown horizon. Good-bye Lakehurst, New Jersey, good-bye!

....

MAPS TO
ANYWHERE

How to Draw

I'm going to demonstrate how to draw, but first let me say that despite several years of a fine arts education, including extensive classes on the history of world art (with an emphasis on contemporary American art), and after learning all I possibly could about the human impulse to make images—from horses on the walls in the caves at Lascaux to the patterns dug in the desert by the man who began the earthworks movement—I possess, against every cultivated judgment which came with my master's degree, a fondness for amateur art. As far as I'm concerned, any novice's doodle of the human body—its hasty face and improbable proportions—is as good as if not better than half the paintings that have come out of Soho in the last five years. I mean, if art is a sincere expression of emotions and ideas, who is doing a better job, the professional artist, commerce in mind, who cranks out a neo-expressionist figure as dull as a fifth-generation xerox, or Mrs. Minn, who lives on my street and every Christmas presents to each neighbor a little Santa, his head askew, made of styrofoam balls and scraps of felt? You'd have to see her ingenuous expression to know exactly what I mean. She's timid yet proud regarding her creations, the weight of good will accompanying her gift undiminished year after year.

Spin Art, popular at county fairs and church bazaars, is a particular favorite of mine. Watching people squeeze paint from those pliable ketchup dispensers onto a revolving canvas reminds me how the abstract expressionists, Pollock in particular, yearned for a process of making art where the pigment had a life of its own, subject to speed and gravity and chance. The results of that frantic squirting and turning look like cosmic phenomena: exploding supernovas, swirling stars, comet trails, nebulae.

My dying brother painted by number a picture of the Eiffel Tower. But the tower listed slightly to the left, the spire seemed to curl, and the final effect was one of fatigue wilting the wonders of the world. Even *The Scream* by Edvard Munch, with its swooning landscape and lurid color, pales in comparison, or should I say diminishes in pitch, a mere murmur when considered against this work by my brother.

Around the time of my brother's illness I began to take an interest in art, perhaps in the hope it could lead to immortality. Even at the age of twelve, I knew the meaning of "posthumous" from watching movies of artist's lives, Hollywood sagas full of adversity, ridicule, madness: Kirk Douglas as Vincent van Gogh, Charleton Heston as Michelangelo. Take *The Moulin Rouge* starring Mel Ferrer; despite the soft-focus poverty, his moonlit garret in disarray, whenever Lautrec wielded a brush the soundtrack thrived with violins. Grief was transmuted to passion, obsession, and close-ups of an extra's hand making the appropriate, painterly stroke.

My mother adored Toulouse-Lautrec. "And to think," she sighed, "the guy was a midget." She had framed a poster of the Moulin Rouge, the patrons leering, dissipated, cloaked and hunched over amber glasses, the cancan dancers lit from below, their smiles huge and inhuman. She saw in it—or wanted to see—an atmosphere of gaiety, as dense and sweet as creme de menthe, an exotic evening out on the town. That gouache of the raucous demi-monde offered my mother moments of release from a life with her sickly son in the foreground.

I, on the other hand, was transported by minimal art, with its simple, stark geometry, its flawless presence in an unruly world. A copy of *Art Scene* in my junior high library contained a feature on minimalist sculpture. I was fascinated by what I saw, but wondered why so many of those monumental sculptures were called "untilted" when several of them did, in fact, tilt one way or another, some quite precariously, as though they might collapse atop the viewer if he or she so much as sneezed. Soon after I realized my mistake, a minimalist sculpture by Richard Serra, as it was being installed at the Guggenheim Museum, fell and crushed a construction worker. From that point on, the harmlessness of amateur art became one of its chief virtues. No one, to my knowledge, has been killed by a replica of the Jefferson Memorial made out of toothpicks, or a snowflake cut from folded paper, or a poodle composed of pink balloons.

If I were inclined to collect art, I'd want objects made on the spur of the moment by people at bus stops and coffee shops and bars: straws bent into Möbius strips, impromptu paper-napkin puppets, sculpted wads of chewing gum. I'd place *my* address on the back of that matchbook that tells you to draw Binky the Duck and send in the result to be evaluated by an art expert. I bet I'd receive mutations on the mallard that would set Charles Darwin's hair on end. Think of the mail laden with ducks, a room full of variegated Binkys, piles dividing good Binkys from bad.

I've had bad experiences with authoritarian art instructors who came right up, grabbed my charcoal, and ruined what I thought was a good composition. The worst transgressor in this respect was Mrs. Arlington, the seventh grade teacher who told me I'd never master hands—they dangled below the sketchbook's edge; they were held behind the subject's back. Versed in child psychology, she considered each picture a self-portrait, thought my omission problematic, the sign of a stingy temperament. Dear Mrs. Arlington: those hands were present all along, dipped below the threshold of vision, in the netherworld of white paper.

Home from school on hot afternoons, I'd draw on the pavement with a feather dunked in water. I'd start with Mrs. Arlington and watch her image disappear. After that was seared away by the sun, I drew my brother lying in bed, his body fading second by second, molecules sucked invisibly up. And I drew my mother doing the cancan. And I drew myself, handless of course, a mortal boy staring straight ahead.

One afternoon toward the end of his life, my brother spoke

on the phone to his doctor. His voice was weak, the telephone black and oracular. Gary repeated, "Yes, yes," nodding to no one. He absently drew on a pad of paper.

A spiral twisted in or out; it was hard to tell. Jagged stars hovered in a corner, their light a burst of lines. Some random spots were marked with an X. The box could have been a house, and the lumps surrounding it, trees. Or perhaps they were dogs. Or perhaps they were cars. Or perhaps they were shapes for the sake of shape. Superimposed over that scene was the profile of a face—man and woman, young and old—the face of everyone at once.

Days later that sketch was torn off, tossed away, the sheet beneath it embossed with abundance: objects that seemed to be molded from snow, vague symbols rimmed in shadow. Impressions. Perimeters. Ghostly. Gone.

Maps to
Anywhere

The proprietress of Maps to Anywhere begins to spin in her swivel chair. The walls are covered with time zones and oceans, the room filled with dozens of globes scattered in shafts of dusty sunlight. She grips the seat and shoves off the floor to propel herself faster and faster. Her head tilts back. Her eyes close. The million lavender threads of her sweater swathe her like an atmosphere. She sings a song about strange places, an anthem improvised under her breath:

> Oh, Yalta and Bulgaria,
> dum, dum, la, la, la,
> Oahu and . . . Mozambique . . .
> Helsinki and . . . Baja.

Despite her stock of atlases, it's safe to say this woman is lost, at least for several delirious minutes. She doesn't even notice that I'm standing at the door.

Whenever I've dropped a cufflink or a key and groped on the floor unable to find it, I could feel the world turn, buildings dimming in the dusk, the continent slipping into the dark, the planet trapped like a roast on a rotisserie, relentless rotations of night and day. Within this onslaught of time, I'd reach beneath the dresser, the bed, stirring up flimsy galaxies of dust, retrieving nothing, astonished and alone.

The whirling proprietress puts on the brakes, digs her high heels into the carpet. She tries to steady her lavender torso, clutches her churning head in her hands. Maps to everywhere must be in motion, latitudes and longitudes undulating before her eyes, hundreds of small pastel countries whizzing by like pricked balloons, the names of rivers and towns and mountains smeared and indecipherable.

A minute passes. Nothing but the shush of traffic and motes tumbling through shafts of light.

"Sorry," she blurts, blushing up at me. Wobbling, cordial, she rises from her chair, straightens her collar, smooths her skirt. "Mazel," she says, extending her hand, "Mrs. Mazel. And how may I help you?"

Her hand in mine is soft and hot. "I'm looking for a globe. Just something simple. How about those?" I point to a group of globes on the floor.

"Replogle globes. Model two-fourteen." She furrows her forehead, bites her lip. "Nice. But the colors are dull, don't you think?"

Before I can answer, Mrs. Mazel has crossed the room, her blonde bouffant as big as the sun among these excess earths.

"Now this," she says, "is the Dexter Special." She holds up a heavier, darker globe, raps her knuckle along its equator. That world resounds with a muffled thud. "Solid. Comes with a two-year warranty. Guaranteed not to dent or fade."

I've made up my mind. The Replogle is perfect. But Mrs. Mazel is over in a corner, jumping at a globe on the highest shelf. It almost drops as she drags it down. Walking briskly back to me, she grazes an entire table of globes which creak through a chorus of revolutions.

"Feel it," she says, thrusting this one up to my face. "Close your eyes and feel it."

"Mrs. Mazel, I'm in a hurry."

The planet before me starts to sink, and there, huge behind it, is the face of Mrs. Mazel.

"I wanted to be of assistance," she whispers.

There have been mornings, walking to work, when the heads of pedestrians looked like planets, every face encased in its weather, flushed cheeks, cold noses, all that shifting geography, the mumbling lips, the nervous tics. Today I get stranded on planet Mazel. Her topography amazes me: hazel eyes enmeshed in wrinkles, large dark nostrils, pointed chin.

I look to make sure that no one is watching and I wipe my palms on my woolen pants and I close my eyes and I feel the globe till I reach a part that's raised.

"What a relief," jokes Mrs. Mazel, her voice deep from cigarettes. "And what mountain range is that?" she asks, slowly, as though I'm her hopeless pupil. She tilts the peaks to meet my fingers. I can hear her breathing through her nose. "Now keep those eyes of yours closed," she intones. "No cheating allowed, Mr. ———?"

The world feels chilly and sad and small, metallic and hollow and inconsequential, and I can't, for the life of me, recollect my name, or the name of the minuscule mountain range plunged into darkness beneath my palm. I let my right index finger fall off a shallow coast and flounder. Whatever ocean this is, is calm, except for an archipelago's braille, abstract and hard as rock.

"Stone," I can barely hear myself say. From far away, from within the dark, I lie. "Mr. Stone."

Mrs. Mazel keeps turning the world, very carefully, around and around. Strange terrain slides under my hands. My fingers, reaching beyond the horizon, are swept by the trade winds of Mrs. Mazel's breath.

I have to pry my eyes open, and what I find is blinding: Mrs. Mazel standing before me and beaming with authority. I'd forgotten how this place is cramped, typewriters shrouded in plastic covers, stacks of mail about to topple. It seems like days since I passed through that door.

"This is my lunch hour, Mrs. Mazel. Please, pack the Replogle."

Mrs. Mazel turns quickly officious. She scoops a globe up off the floor. She drops my purchase into a box, presses in crescents of styrofoam which squeak like tiny lives in pain. "There," she announces, handing me the box. Its sides are bulging. "Will that be cash or charge, Mr. Stone?"

Last week they drained the Echo Park lake and every possession I'd ever lost seemed to be strewn in its muddy dregs: an algae-covered credit card, a fountain pen, puckered shoes. And radiating out from the lake were palm trees posted with notices: missing parrot, blue and orange, eats sunflower seeds, answers to "George"; schnauzer, big, shy, reward; calico kitten with white paws, blind in one eye, please call. On the road, traffic roared and retreated. On the sidewalk, newspapers blew away. All things on earth were lost or leaving.

Walking back to work with the globe, I'm jostled by people who rush toward the park to claim a place on the grass to have lunch. The winter sun is low but warm. Everyone wants to feel it on their faces. They all crane in the same direction, planets leaning their cheeks to the light. And there at the center of their basking lies the lake, filled again, clear as a mirror. Huge, fluid clouds move through it, blown to Brussels, Paraguay, Perth.

Utopia

Today I was going to borrow some books about mankind's concepts of utopia, but the downtown library was destroyed by fire a couple of months ago and now there is only a charred hull, stepped like a ziggurat, cordoned off at a busy intersection, soot seeping from its broken windows, the whole block reeking of smoke. I thought of going to another library, but that would involve negotiating unfamiliar streets, and I'm a man entrenched in routine. I travel the city like a needle coursing through grooves of a record. Work, market, home. Work, market, home. You visit the same places often enough and each day is like the refrain of Old Black Magic—"Round and round I go, in a spin, loving that spin I'm in . . ."

When I look back at childhood, my breakfast bowl was like the curved congress building in the South American capital of Brasilia, a city whose stark architecture was eventually overrun with clotheslines and curtains and chickens plodding through lobbies. The spotless glass-topped bureau where my mother and father kept cologne and lint brushes and shoehorns was a lot like Le Corbusier's Radiant City, egalitarian, rational, based upon the symmetry of His and Hers. Except that my parents filed for divorce. Except that Corbu's schematic plans are nothing now but a blur of monoliths rendered in pencil. Our yard was like a small model of Frank Lloyd Wright's Broadacre City; the faulty fountain, wooden birdhouse, and sparse vegetable garden were as absurd as Wright's metropolis where each resident, living in a mile-high apartment complex, would own an individual plot of farmland which they could fly to in a compact helicopter adorned with geometric designs.

Anyway, I ended up staying at home today, crossing the carpet on journeys to the window and desk and back, staring at tract houses which cover the hills like ice plant or ivy, redundant and dense. As a boy, I used to visit a local subdivision every Sunday and wander through the model home. The foyer was filled with piped-in music. I'd swing back a medicine cabinet mirror to reveal the pristine enamel, the green tiers of glass. Nubby synthetic curtains, clamped tight against the view, created a dim monastic light just right for contemplation. One need only pull a cord to, swoosh, be blinded by the wall of a neighbor, shadowless and absolute across a dusty abyss. Even the brochure's abbreviations—2 bdrm., 2 ba., fully equip. kit.— sounded primal, percussive, melodic as a conga. Late at night the tract homes twinkled, windows burnished by the television's glow, pool lights bluing the air, electric garage doors yawning. And I would have given anything to be the boy in my illustrated school book, walking up to a typical house that contained a family, open-armed, ebullient with the usual greeting.

My home life resisted perfection, and I vented my frustration on Plasticville, an HO-scale community consisting of a fire station, hospital, airport, market, post office, school, ranch house, and cottage. I'd orchestrate train wrecks in the heart of town, or instigate earthquakes, just to see the microcosm topple, to force walls to shake from foundations, to cause bright pieces to fall where they may. But this was nothing compared to the documentary I'd seen of a house in the Nevada desert where Mr. and Mrs. Mannequin and their kids waited in a living room to test the effects of a nuclear blast. Those splintering chairs, that melting hair, those bodies blown like dust from erasers . . .

I can't possibly go about my business day in and day out, parting the curtain of space before me, with any greater sense of apocalypse than I already have. Why, just a few days ago I watched this program on TV where an archaeologist who had unearthed more bodies in Pompeii pulled out trays of remains she actually had pet names for. "Octavia," she said, waving a clavicle. And then she rummaged through the rest of the bones in much the same way that I used to rummage through the puzzle pieces of an autumn landscape searching for the red parts of the barn.

For years, I loved the lightest, most makeshift of shelters: the tent of a linen sheet that sifted the afternoon light; the dining table's underworld with its pillars of living legs. This was long before I'd heard of Buckminster Fuller's comprehensive-anticipatory-design-science, or laid eyes upon a geodesic dome, a habitat of facets as complex as a diamond, though not as enduring. This was before the advent of megastructures composed of lightweight, prefabricated, single-family units which were piled into place by stupendous cranes. This was before the international housing shortage when major urban areas were left to decay and bands of adolescents with shaved heads and black jackets would rasp lyrics like, "Home is where the heart is. Home is so remote. Home is just emotion sticking in my throat."

Morning after morning I listen to music. This morning I played a record of Debussy's "The Sunken Cathedral." For eight minutes and twenty-two seconds, those subaquatic octaves formed in my mind a conception of refuge so sweet, I felt as though I were living in Atlantis; treble and bass had the tensile strength of lintels and beams; the grand piano hammered chords that rose up higher and higher. And as the finale filled the room, sound waves pummeled the plaster walls, molecules tumbling down by the billions.

....

THE WIND
DID IT

Sleeping with My Father

My father glances at an airplane in the distance and tells me this story as he drives down the street:

"Remember when Mrs. King lived next door? Well, she used to work as a chaperone for *The Dating Game,* and one day a couple won a trip to Israel and she went with them. TWA I think it was. And she told me that toward the end of the flight a stewardess comes over to where the three of them are sitting and asks would they move back a few rows. So they do, kind of confused, and then these Israelis in uniform come out of the cockpit, dismantle some seats, set up machine guns and aim them out the windows. Mrs. King—remember how nice she was?—anyway, she got very upset. Who wouldn't? And she says to the stewardess, she says, 'Dear, level with me. What's with the ammo?' and the stewardess says, 'Just a precautionary measure. Terrorists. You know. . . . We've never had cause to fire.'"

"Dad," I ask, "did you believe her?"

"Tell me, Mr. Skeptic," he says, lifting both hands from the steering wheel in order to shrug his shoulders, "why would a stewardess lie?"

"No," I moan. "Did you believe Mrs. King?"

My father blinks, remains silent. He adjusts his glasses, the broken stem held together by a clot of electrical tape. His white hair gleams with Brylcreem.

"Look, Pop," I say, "if the windows of the airplane were open, all the passengers, Mrs. King included, would be sucked into the stratosphere. Poof. Gone."

"Yeah, yeah. Maybe you have a point. It's a good story, though." He flicks a switch marked AIR, and in seconds the inside of the car is arctic. "I don't know why I brought it up," he says. "I was just thinking. I was just looking back."

For nearly a year, my father has been divorced from his second wife, Esther, a black elementary-school teacher and devout Catholic forty years his junior. She has yet to retrieve her possessions from his house, the Spanish house in which I grew up, its walls and vestibules still crowded with their combined religious artifacts: his statuette of Moses in windblown robes, hoisting the Ten Commandments; her oil painting of Jesus gazing heavenward, pious, pale. Crosses and stars of David vie for attention in every room. These, combined with heavy Mediterranean furniture, give his house an inquisitional air.

During his three-year marriage to Esther, my father and I rarely saw each other. In an attempt to "turn over a new leaf," as he so often put it, he summarily jettisoned from his life those people and things that bound him to the past: my mother's jewelry—she'd made no provision for it in her will—was pawned; the house was repainted a pale chartreuse with chocolate trim (Mrs. King would have been appalled); and as for me, his thirty-five-year-old baby, I was, so to speak, tossed out with the bath water. Once, though, I ran into him at the supermarket, his "new leaf" manifest in a little dance I saw him do down the aisle: he swayed in rhythm behind the cart as he grabbed at cinnamon coffee cake, tubes of juice, bags of Esther's favorite candy, Muzak humming into the air from some lofty, mysterious source—the ceiling, the spheres; it didn't matter. Dad was entranced in a dance of veils, burdens flung from his aging body.

These idyllic days were numbered, however. Unlike my father, Esther brought with her to the marriage the full force of her past, a hidden past which included bouts of depression, a melancholy undiminished by regimens of exercise or psychotropic drugs. She spent weeks languishing in bed, mute and inconsolable, her jaw clenched, the shades drawn. Just how my father dealt with Esther's descent into despair—and finally rage—I'm not certain, but I know my father well enough to speculate that he must have tickled her, crooned songs, made faces, regaled her with gifts, utterly mystified as to why his kindness and cajoling had no effect. His new wife was deaf to his entreaties. Her tempting figure was wrapped in blankets, her eyes extinguished. He interpreted Esther's condition as an affront, proof that his reserves of playfulness, his romantic machinations would come to nothing, proof that, in the end, the troubled life he tried to escape could not be pawned or painted away.

His past washed back, and I rode with it.

More and more these days I keep him company. He'll drive us to Art's Prime Rib, his favorite restaurant, and always we seem to head toward the sun. The visors are no help; a glare, intense and tropical, saturates his Cadillac, and there, at the end of the street, the summer sun consumes the horizon, branding hotspots on the Caddy's hood.

I've never told him that I read the article about his divorce suit in the *Herald Examiner*. His claims against Esther must have struck the reporter as sufficiently preposterous to warrant space under Local News. The headline read, "One for the Three Bears: Suit Filed in Bed Rights Fight." The copy spared no details:

> Attorney Edward S. Cooper's wife didn't take kindly to his decision to retire for the night in her bedroom, according to a $25,000 lawsuit Cooper filed against Mrs. Cooper yesterday. In fact, Cooper said, his wife, Esther Williams Cooper, brandished a 12-inch knife, punched him repeatedly and smashed his eyeglasses while demanding that he get out. As a result, Cooper's suit contends, the attorney suffered "severe shock . . . severe pain in the right ear . . . is in fear of becoming totally deaf, thereby losing his right to earn his livelihood from his profession." He also suffered a groin injury and a cut under his left eye.
>
> According to the Superior Court action, the assault took place on July 9, when Mrs. Cooper found her

eighty-year-old husband sleeping in her bedroom of
their Hollywood home. The Coopers had occupied
separate bedrooms since May 30, the suit said.

I offer the above excerpt not as evidence of the humiliation
my father no doubt endured when this article appeared, nor
as a way of substantiating events that might otherwise seem
exaggerated for literary effect; rather, I offer it so that one might
better understand how, as my father and I drive to dinner, my
secret knowledge of him, acquired via the news, hangs between
us like a crystal chandelier, swaying and clinking, erupting with
refractions.

My father's history can be divided into three distinct
phases. During my boyhood and his marriage to my mother
until her death, my father was a man wracked by an excess of
energy. He never seemed to sleep. His was not the insomnia that
results in indolence, bags beneath the eyes, stifled yawns. When
he was awake he was *wide* awake, jumping at the slightest noise.
No exertion, regardless how back-breaking, could exhaust him
completely. On Sundays, he gardened our yard till sunset, un-
shaven and glazed with sweat. Nights were devoted to pacing,
a record of his aimless trails and quick pivots crushed into the
carpet. He brought work home from his office by the armload,
teetering stacks of depositions, dog-eared files. He even ate in
nervous surges, spearing and gulping, his face flushed, the veins
in his temples blue. Sometimes my mother and I would balk at
his fervor, our own forkfuls frozen mid-air, and we'd stare at
each other and then at my father who'd grumble "What," his
mouth still full.

The next, or newlywed period, was, as I've mentioned, char-
acterized by abandon, buoyancy, boyishness. The blood that had
once banged through his heart had somehow turned to helium.
On my way home from work once, I saw my father's Cadillac
parked in the lot of the local florists, and I pictured him offering
blossoms to Esther, beaming above a prodigious bouquet. Apart

from flowers and his dance to Muzak, let the following list of objects stand for this phase of my father's life: a cassette of Tony Bennett's greatest hits, a pair of Sergio Valenti jeans with gold piping, a cherrywood box in which were kept the corks he'd coaxed from bottles of champagne.

The third and current phase began after he made the *Herald*. It is, to me, the most astonishing of all. Yes, he is lonely, remorseful, baffled at dawn in his infamous bed. Strangely though, he is never despondent, but talkative, gentle, tempered by troubles. Without warning or preamble, without so much as clearing his throat, he'll launch into some story, the gist of which is comparison, comparison for its own sweet sake:

"See that dog food billboard? Well, once my brother and I had a dog. A schnauzer. Brown. Sammy or something . . ."

"And . . . ?"

"That's it, boychik. I was just thinking. I was just looking back."

Driving to dinner with my father is like entering a chamber in which Then and Now collide and coalesce, the narrative equivalent of nuclear fusion. This dreamy world view of his is infectious, and I've caught myself more than once gazing out the car window, engaged in thoughts that vacillate between the present and the past, ending finally in pleasant limbo between the two. I've also noticed that my father and I are starting to look and sound alike. Our voices share a Semitic inflection, each bit of banter rising slightly, every sentence becoming a question. Should we pass some lunatic flailing his arms and orating on the corner, we'll both expel a breath of air and slap our cheeks in disbelief. My hair is receding just as his did. We each have long lashes, clefts in our chins, a mole at the base of our throats. Maybe it's the blazing sun that accentuates the traits we share.

In those moments when we've nothing left to talk about, I imagine that my father and I, heat-baked, squinting, will ride together to the end of the earth, the car careening toward the center of the sun, our lives ignited in a sudden conflagration, our fates melded in a blast of light.

I had a dream about my father. I dreamed it after his divorce from Esther, after his loneliness became clear to me, after he'd begun to tell meandering stories, after we'd shared a few dinners together, after I'd begun to recognize the ways in which we're alike. I came to him in his bedroom. He was sleeping in the center of a double bed. The room was suffused with blue light. It was dusk or dawn, I didn't know. On the dresser, statuettes of Moses and Jesus oversaw our assignation. I stroked his shoulder. My father awoke. "Dad," I whispered, "are we getting older?" "Here," he said, lifting the blanket. "Here," he said, patting the bed.

Machu Picchu

Since his divorce from Esther, my father has read *Secrets of the Maya* five times. The paperback lies like a Bible on his nightstand. I've yet to ask him how his obsession with the Maya began, but my rare ventures into his bedroom during the past year have yielded a theory. Esther redecorated the room in a vivid collision of colors—orange afghan, purple lamp shades, wallpaper flocked with blue flowers—which no doubt intensify my father's insomnia. And this paperback book, with its tales of the ancients playing handball, inventing calendars, climbing the steps of pyramids, offers my father hours of escape from a room that vibrates with Esther's presence.

Still, it's only a theory, and tonight over dinner at Art's Prime Rib, I ask my father if he would try to articulate just what it is about this particular civilization that intrigues him. For a moment he appears not to hear me and continues to blow on a spoonful of soup. Then he looks up. Thick glasses magnify his eyes. He pushes his French onion soup aside, places his palms on the table.

"First of all," he says, "they worshiped everything there was to worship, like, um, corn . . ." He drums his fingers, stumped. "You know—things . . . buildings. And they made contributions to the societies of today, like x-ray."

"X-ray?"

"Yeah. Well, not x-ray. But they carved stone pictures of people's insides. Pregnant women and where their babies would be, or just your average Mayas with lungs and livers. Now I'm not saying that these were actual x-rays as we know them, but you have to start somewhere, right? I mean, how'd they think of these things? Shirley McLaine, the actress, the one who wrote that book *Tree* something . . ."

"*Out on a Limb.*"

My father snaps his fingers. "Limb, that's it. Anyway, she thinks the Mayas and Aztecs and Incas were advanced people from another planet. I'm not saying I believe her, see, but it *is* food for thought. Boychik," he adds, plucking a radish from a bowl of ice, "the world is full of unanswered questions."

The waiter appears with our salads. He dangles a pepper mill over the table. My father waves it away.

Silence punctuated by the crunch of lettuce.

"Hey," he blurts. "How'd you like to visit Machu Picchu with me?"

"Machu Picchu?"

"Whadd'ya say we go there. Together." My father leans forward, his expression so sincere, his voice so plaintive, I think he might try to kiss me. "The Lost City," he says. His moist eyes catch the candlelight.

I can't answer my father immediately; I'm dizzy with mountain peaks, black and green, slicing huge and fluid clouds, the air so thin it muffles sound. Even parrots avoid this height. My father sits on a crumbling wall, holding his knees and breathing hard. "Oy," he heaves. "We're actually here. Give the donkeys something to drink."

The steam from a mound of mashed potatoes eases me out of my fantasy. As tempting as his offer sounds, as much as it appeals to my desire to be, for the first time, his loyal son, I've never taken a trip alone with my father, and to attempt one now might jeopardize the intimacy we've recently achieved.

"Nice that you asked, Dad. But I really can't afford it."

"Afford? I'll pay."

"I . . . my classes."

"Summer then."

"I teach in the summer, too."

"O.K.," he says. He turns up his hearing aid and flinches at its high-pitched whistle. "You can't say I didn't try."

"I ought to get rid of this place," my father says when we return from dinner. He fumbles for the key to the door. "It's too damn big for one person." Behind us in the driveway, the Cadillac ticks as the engine cools. "Ta-da," Dad sings when he finds the right key.

There are in my life a small number of sensations which never seem to vary or diminish: a sudden chill at the sight of blood, numbness in the legs induced by heights. To these may be added the sensation of entering my father's house, the odors layered and playing like music: a counterpoint of plastic and wood, a musty undertone coming from the rugs, my father's lemon aftershave resounding within the walls.

I follow my father as he moves through the rooms and flicks on the lights. "I need all this?" he asks, pointing with both arms around the large living room. We sit opposite each other on identical velvet couches. I shrug and investigate the objects crowded on the coffee table: a souvenir brochure from John F. Kennedy's inauguration, a book of paintings by Norman Rockwell, an album with photos of my father and Esther, suntanned, smiling. "Dad," I ask, "where were these pictures taken?"

"Mexico," he mutters. He stares over my head and out the bay window. Twilight bathes his upturned face, accentuates lines and shadows. "Honeymoon," he continues, without looking at me. "Mayas." My father remains mesmerized for what seems like minutes, his body perfectly still, eyes fixed on some distant point. Dust motes drift through the air between us. Finally his gaze meets mine. "I'm stuffed," he says, patting his stomach. "How 'bout TV?"

We lumber upstairs to his bedroom, where my father keeps a wide-screen Zenith. He opens a window, settles into a recliner and fiddles with the remote control. I sit near his feet. On *Jeopardy*, Alex Trebek, the game show's host, is reminding the three contestants that they will be shown answers, and must phrase their response in the form of a question.

"Jeez this game is tough," my father says. "I hardly ever get one right." He has strapped an electric massager to his hand. It begins to buzz. He touches his vibrating hand to my head. I shiver and arch my back against his knees. My father rakes his fingers through my hair, presses my scalp until everything trembles—the people on the screen, the table and ottoman flanking the set, the flowers flocked on the wall. My glasses slowly slide down my nose. Colors are jolted from the edges of objects, the room blurred and otherworldly. I worry I may lose control, begin to whimper or weep with pleasure.

"What is euthanasia?" screams my father. "Who was Woodrow Wilson?" He traces concentric circles on my temples, squeezes the nape of my neck. My ears are hot, my shoulders succumb to gravity. "What is a microchip? Who are the Mormon Tabernacle Choir? What is penicillin?" From the corner of my eye, through the shaking window, I see the jostled tops of trees, the quivering peaks of the Hollywood hills, faint stars wobbling in the sky. My father continues to work down my spine, calling questions into the night.

Father as Fountain

"No," says my father, "it wasn't my appendix." He changes lanes without looking.

"Kidney stones?" I ask. "Gall bladder?"

"For the life of me," says my father, smacking his forehead, "I can't remember what they took out of me. Whatever the hell it was, Bernard, I've felt a lot better these past few months." The Caddy's electric windows whir down. My father's baggy Hawaiian shirt flutters in the breeze.

"Have you lost weight, Dad?"

My father tries to look at his torso. "Maybe a little," he says. "The food the maid cooks is pretty bad. She cleans up beautiful though. I've still got to lose more. Doctor's orders."

Burning at the center of our discourse like the sun is the one subject we never miss, the subject which dwarfs and outshines all the others: the state of our health. We carefully monitor every ache and crimp and itch. We talk about our blocked sinuses, fallen arches, ingrown hairs.

"Look at this red thing on my wrist," my father says at a stoplight.

"Oh, that's just a cherry angioma."

"A what?"

"Like a mole. But red. It's nothing."

"How do you . . . ?"

"*Scribner's Dictionary of Medical Terms.* I'll get you a copy."

"You don't think it's . . ."

"Everybody has them. Believe me. I looked it up."

My father checks once more to be sure. He holds his wrist close to his face as though he were sampling a dab of cologne.

Our mutual fascination with the body and the countless ailments that might besiege it was brought about, in part, by my mother's lifelong obsession with nutrition. She bought every book that extolled the virtues of vitamins, herbal remedies, or novel diets—*Rice for Life, Food Groups and You, A Practical Guide to Cooking with Parsley.* She once read that chopping vegetables breaks down their cellular structure to such an extent that the minerals are virtually useless. For weeks after, my father and I were served, on pink plates, whole carrots (tops included), plump zucchinis, and bell peppers. When she read that Jewish folk wisdom was confirmed by doctors who found that chicken broth did, in fact, help cure colds, she had the kosher butcher deliver a trio of plucked and pale fowl. For years, on the advice of nutritionist Adele Davis, she plied my father and me with gallons of milk for healthy marrow. My mother was inconsolable when she heard that Adele Davis had died from bone cancer. She didn't mourn the woman herself. Rather, my mother mourned the hope that somewhere among the pages of her books was hidden the secret of sustenance, the key to our longevity.

All my relatives, to varying degrees, were preoccupied with physical well-being. Even as a child, when my parents played bridge with Aunt Flo and Uncle Sid, I'd be curled on the living-room couch, surfacing from a mild sleep to hear them whisper the strange words I sensed meant something bad about the body —*ulcer, lumbago, cataract.* The mention of these afflictions was followed by Father clicking his tongue.

"You've got to live for today," he'd say.

"Live for today," echoed my aunt. "You just never know."

"In the meantime," said Mother, shuffling the cards, "you have to live right."

Sid knocked on the wooden table. "Now, that's a fact."

In those dim, sweet, preconscious days, mortality was still remote, a rumor overheard from the province of adults. And as much as my father feared growing old—"Look at these gray hairs, Lil. They're a different texture altogether"—I believed that he was exempt from time, that his fears would never escalate, his wrinkles never deepen.

"At Cedars," groans my father as we pull into the parking lot, "they make me wait an hour and a half for my blood pressure medicine. Jeez, it makes me so mad I think I might get a heart attack right there. What's the stuff that you take, boychik?"

As we walk into Art's and wait to be seated for an early dinner, I tell my father about hydrochlorothiazide, proud that I can pronounce it, proud, even, that the pressure of our blood unites us. Swept up in a mood of camaraderie, of confidentiality, a mood intensified by the dim lighting, red walls, eclairs revolving in the pastry case, I share with my father the story of how, when I first took hydrochlorothiazide, I had a dream—my doctor warned me it might affect my dreams—in which I was fed glucose intravenously while being rolled down an alley on a gurney by a dozen identical Amazon women on roller skates who wore zebra-skin bikinis and told me they were taking me for an audience with their leader, a blind Las Vegas lounge singer, his pompadour oily and black.

My father is silent. He looks away. I panic that my story was inappropriate, that my father considers strange dreams a sign of instability, that I've made a fool of myself and put a dent in our burgeoning relationship.

"Dad," I say, blushing, "that drug is really strong. The doctor said . . ."

"Prostate," shouts my father. The hostess looks up from her clipboard. Two blue haired women sitting in club chairs narrow their eyes. A man in Sans-A-Belt slacks peers in our direction. My father slaps his thigh and smiles. "They took out my prostate. I knew it would come to me sooner or later."

It's still eighty degrees out when we get back to my father's house. "How 'bout a swim?" he says. "I'll get the scuba gear. Ha ha."

"I don't have my trunks with me."

"So wear your underpants."

"Only if you do, too."

My father and I stand beside one another in boxer shorts, our toes hanging over the rim of the pool. Pine needles float on the surface of the water. A drowning bee flails in circles.

"You first," I say.

"What?" he says. He's taken out his hearing aid.

"I said, You first."

"You."

"You."

There has been, these summer evenings, a clear, incomparable cast of light, the air dry and slightly golden. It laves my father's pale body and he takes on that subtle strain of gold. Without his glasses, he cranes his face forward, eyes shining. The white hair on his chest and arms throws a profusion of tangled shadows. His belly protrudes like a little boy's. His knees are chapped and the skin is loose. His feet bear the ribbed impression of his socks.

"When you were just a baby," he says, gazing into the water, "you and your mom and I were out here, and she and I were talking, and we turned around and you were gone. Then mother pointed at the pool. I swear you were down there, right on the bottom, blowing out bubbles, not crying or kicking, just looking up. Boy, was I scared, and I dove in and got you." My father looks at me. He puts his hand on my shoulder. "I don't suppose you remember that?"

"No," I say as he shoves me in the pool.

When I resurface, I see my father, arms outstretched, falling toward me, a look of blind abandon on his face. He hits the churning waves with a smack and springs up flinging water from his arms. He makes motor boat noises and plows his fist across the pool. He does an awkward handstand, skinny legs weaving through the air, hairs matted to calves. I'm in the deep end, treading water. "Look," he yells, turning profile. He dunks himself under, emerges with his cheeks full. He holds out his arms, hands bent back at a graceful angle, fingers splayed. A thin, silver jet of water shoots from the space between his two front teeth. It arches a yard in front of him, sputters and dwindles away.

"What am I?" he shouts, laughing and splashing.

"A fountain," I say, amazed.

Horseradish
(Lessons in Pleasure and Pain)

I learned from my father that pleasure can merge with pain. The catalyst for my new knowledge was horseradish. Dad usually consumed it with Mother's boiled beef or gefilte fish, but in this instance it was eaten alone, directly from a condiment jar, with a tiny silver spoon. My father and I were squeezed into the breakfast nook, waiting for dinner, empty plates before us. The sun was going down; I looked out the kitchen window and tried to see the night happen. I must have worn the distant expression I was known for as a child. Even mother's puttering —nibbling brisket, lifting lids—couldn't disrupt my concentration. I'm not sure when my hungry father inserted the spoon in his mouth. All I recall is the guttural noise, low at first, as though it came from outside the house, tugging me from my reverie. But the groan was deep in my father's throat, growing in volume, borne on the air, resounding in the room. And then I saw the silver spoon as he slid it out of his mouth.

My father knocked on his head with his fist, whined like a whistle, fanned his face. My father shuddered and pounded the table. His eyes were wide and red and wet from the sting of spice, the heat of the root. He gulped water to no avail. He sucked ice but that was futile. He tilted his head from side to side. Cartilage cracked. He blew his nose in a paper napkin. "God," he blurted, "is that ever good."

Mother turned from the stove and observed these antics with mild amusement. She shook her head. But something opened inside of me, some realization which, like my father's enjoyment, was burning and sweet at the same time. I couldn't think of any word for what I understood. Had I been pressed to describe it, I would have said that black and white can mix together, but remain black and white even though they make grey. There were, I sensed, other similar phenomena in the world: day and night, mother and father, happy and sad, in tandem and yet forever apart. Soon after that dinner, there followed several occurrences, featuring Father, which demonstrated the principle of pleasure hand in hand with pain.

The first involved the wrestler Gorgeous George. My father was a devout fan. Seated in a wing chair three feet away from our blond TV, he jumped up when George was victorious, cursed when George was pinned to the mat. If you watched my father on those Saturday nights, you'd think it was he who was being pummeled. He grabbed his throat during every half nelson, rolled with the blows when contenders were struck. He didn't, for a minute, believe that the competition was real. He knew that Gorgeous George—who wore a purple cape into the ring and primped his long, bleached hair—was coached to brag and flex and strut. And yet Father flinched and covered his eyes, yeowling in vicarious pain while his shoulders shook with laughter.

The second occurrence took place late one night on my way downstairs to get a glass of water. The rooms of the house were shot with moonlight cold as marble. Their door was ajar, their blanket heaving. A flash of my father's back. A glint of my mother's ring. Silence erupting with an utterance—his or hers I didn't know—that blended the sense of yes and no, the tones of yielding and protestation. And that was all, except for a snap of static when I touched the wrought-iron banister.

Though his doctor has given express instructions that my father avoid spicy food, he sometimes sneaks a dollop of horseradish. It may be the meager quantity that modifies his reaction. He may feel self-conscious at Art's Prime Rib, familiar as he is with the waitresses and waiters. Or perhaps the taste of horseradish has lost some of its zing. Whatever the reason, when my father scoops up a purple daub and touches it to his tongue, his eyes faintly water, his adam's apple bobs, the ghost of a smile shivers on his lips. "Yum," he says with brevity.

Before my father was married to Esther, he called me one night to ask for help. His voice was barely audible. Something about a pain in his side. I rushed to his house, letting myself in the front door with a key I hadn't used in years. I searched the rooms, calling and calling. I found him in pajamas, doubled up on the bathroom floor. His face was a knot. When he looked up, I felt I'd been struck by a gust of his pain.

I slid him into his pants and shirt, guiding his arms and spindly legs, softly repeating "There we go." When I buttoned him up, my face was inches away from his. I saw a collision of gratitude and shame that he worked his mouth to talk about. No sound came out. "You're fine," I said.

In the back seat of my car, headed for the emergency room— that's when the full hurt flooded his stomach. He clutched himself and called for God. I could see him in the rearview mirror, contorted and shining with sweat.

Later, after Dr. Henley diagnosed kidney stones, my father was tucked beneath a blanket and given a dose of Demerol. Together in a makeshift room—folding walls of gathered fabric —I held his hand, though I doubt he knew. Fluorescent light sputtered down like snow. His forehead grew cool. He tested words and slurred, his swallowing loud and dry. "Like having a baby. I couldn't bear . . ." and then he stared at the sound-proof ceiling, the hundred holes like inverse stars. His muscles uncoiled and he breathed in relief. The pain that was building inside him became a portal my father stepped through.

As for pleasure, my father finds it these days in a prank, something he saw long ago in a movie, a prank he pulls when we dine together, a prank he never tires of; it makes him feel sly and quick and clever, proud he can make me break into laughter. Sylvie, the sixty-year-old hostess at Art's—a living mask of stiff hair, penciled eyebrows, crimson lips—grabs two leatherette menus as soon as she sees us coming. From behind a mahogany podium, Sylvie emerges in a knitted dress—painted on, my father says—pink pastel with angora cuffs. "Boys," she coos, pivoting on a high heel, swinging her hips, "walk this way." And my father takes her literally, slinks behind her with tiny steps, head thrown back, hips liquid.

The Wind Did It

Jeopardy flickers on the wide-screen Zenith. The sound is down. My father is packing clothes for Samoa. Gauzy shirts, white trousers, plaid shorts. Using a method as complex as origami, he folds them into compact squares and pats them into the suitcase lying open on his bed. He moves with great deliberation, standing back to look at what he's packed as though he were painting a picture. He fills a shaving kit with mosquito repellent and suntan oil, and then he adds—just in case—Excedrin, cough drops, Band-Aids, Gas-X, Sudafed, and nasal spray.

I'm sprawled on my back in the middle of the room, picking at strands of plush carpet, wishing I hadn't eaten the cheesecake. But my father wanted to celebrate, to say good-bye with something sweet, and besides, he loves to watch me eat, especially foods his doctor forbids. I lift my head and lean on my elbow. "Say his name one more time."

"Muto Peli, the High Talking Chief of Samoa."

"What's that mean, the High Talking part?"

"He's like a spokesman sort of, an ambassador. I was his lawyer back when you were eight. Remember we took him to Disneyland? You didn't want to walk next to him because he wore mouse ears and a sarong. He laughed at everything—and I mean *everything*—and you told Mother he made you scared."

"How long's it been since you've seen him?"

"Jeez, twenty or something years. The last time I saw him was at a barbecue we had for him here. He drove women wild. The guy was fifty, at least, and fat. He roasted an entire pig on a spit; he'd dug a pit in the lawn, remember? And after we ate, he performed a farewell ceremony. Everyone was watching. He handed your mother and me a shell full of sap from the tappa root. It looked like glue, but sipping the stuff was a big honor. Mother went first. She held it in her mouth a long time, trying to muster the courage to swallow."

Suddenly I remember my mother, helpless surprise in her hazel eyes, lips clamped on the sour taste as she tried to force a grin. I also recall how, all my life, Mother flaunted her plans to leave. Every few months, for secret reasons, my mother threatened to move to the sea. "And honey," she'd tell me, "I'm taking you, too. We'll start our lives all over again. Wouldn't you love to live by the beach?" And often my father would disappear to Lancaster, Indio, Santa Rosa, away on business (he'd swear to my mother), returning with baskets of dried fruit wrapped in yellow cellophane. So relentless was their need to escape that during days of the Santa Anas, I'd imagine my parents walking out the door, swept in different directions by the wind, carried like blossoms on hot air, growing smaller and smaller.

"Samoa," I say. "I can't believe you're really going."

My father flaps his wrinkled arms. "If I have to fly there myself."

We walk downstairs and out to my car. As we hug good-bye our glasses bump. I promise him I'll watch his house, water plants, collect the mail. I'm nervous like I used to be when he'd assign me something big to do and I wanted so badly to do it right I knew I'd do it wrong. Especially on Sundays when he gardened our yard, all grunts and curses and animal exertion. My mother and I would stay in the kitchen. She'd smoke a Lucky and stare into space while I colored at the breakfast table, keeping crayon within the lines. She seemed unaware of my father on those days, except that she'd wince when she heard his voice. Otherwise she was far away, tanning on a stretch of sand. Eventually Father would bellow my name, demanding I get myself out of the house. I'd walk out the door and squint at the sun, waiting for instructions. The worst by far was coiling the hose, a task he claimed I could never do well, though he made me do it again and again. Heavy and green and recalcitrant, the hose would snake in the wrong direction and cramp with kinks I couldn't undo. When I was through it looked like a scribble, and my father would swear and shake his head, glaring at me long and hard, and I felt like nothing but skin and sweat.

Back at my own house, lying in bed, I read and reread the notes I wrote (what my father calls an "idiot list"): how and where to turn on the sprinklers, deactivate his burglar alarm. Moonlight seeps through my bedroom windows. A breeze begins to rattle the leaves. The air turns dry, its particles charged. Later that night when I awake, a neighbor's laundry is blowing off the line and lids from trash cans clatter through the street. Sirens are whining far away. I toss and turn as if on a spit. I throw the blanket onto the floor. Though my father has only been gone a few hours, I decide I'd better check his house.

I can spot chartreuse a block away, and dim windows covered with bars. I park in the driveway and sit a minute. Thirty-two thousand one hundred three—the miles I've traveled in the past four years.

I don't bother to turn on the lights. I glide like a ghost from room to room, barely breathing, touching nothing. My heart is a wind chime spinning in my chest. The house is huge and solitary, all the furniture frosted with moonlight—couches, love seats, ottomans, wing chairs—big, sad, soft confections. Outside, the wind is tearing at the trees. Dogs bark in backyards.

Since Esther left, my father has used his dining-room table as a makeshift desk, eating lunch while he sorts the mail. I stand transfixed by the table's contents. He's hoarded coupons he'll never use—Scotchgard, Lime Away, Lady Clairol—torn from the Sunday *Times*. A yellowed brochure for a Mixmaster blender is open to the last page, its outdated warranty recently signed. There's an advertisement for ginseng capsules. A flyer for a missing child. A note that simply says *See you soon*, signed, *Rose—like the flower*.

These bits of paper he's sorted and stacked congeal into something definitive, final, an immense conception about my father that makes the concepts I'd formed in the past seem feeble and inadequate. And just as the fragments combine and cohere— his erratic love of women and money, his tantrums and dancing and banging blood, our season of feasting on prime rib—just as it all becomes seamless, complete, a branch crashes and breaks my concentration, I hear the wind scour the house.

"How was the chief?" I ask my father on the way to Art's. The Santa Anas still toss the trees.

"Fat as ever," my father says. "I've got slides to prove it. Samoan gals all over him like flies. I wish I could bottle that alteh kocker's secret."

"And the flight back, how was that?"

"Like a roller coaster at Coney Island. Thank God for Drama-mine."

"Your plants?" I ask.

"Green as can be. But Bernard," he says, shifting in the seat, "something was wrong when I got back home."

My breath catches and lifts my ribs.

"Nothing's missing. Everything's there. But the front door was wide open."

"Oy," I gasp. "I'm *sure* I closed it." I'm really not sure but I say it twice. My face is hot. I try to fashion some excuse. I brace myself for a reprimand.

"It was kind of strange," my father says, gazing ahead, per-fectly calm. "The door to the house just open like that. Anyone could've walked right in. Leaves and sunlight pouring through. It was fresh inside and . . . I don't know. Maybe, boychik, the wind did it."

AULD LANG SYNE

. . . .

Live Wire

One afternoon, a telephone wire that had hummed in the heat
began to unravel, and the children playing beneath it screamed,
dodged the black tendril that sprang toward the earth, and dazed
parents drew back drapes, peered from windows, swung open
doors, the bright braid of exposed copper scraping the sidewalk,
erupting with sparks, everyone watching them flare and die,
flare and die, the thrashing coil almost alive, and no one spoke,
and all stood still, each child and adult, eyes reflecting a swarm
of sparks, each heard a voice, crackling with static, spill into the
air, surging from that severed end, driven from a distance which
couldn't be explained, coming from a common past, before a
single word was learned, and the night air turned amniotic,
streets extended like arteries, everyone quiet, everyone amazed,
everyone certain they'd heard their name.

Under Water

We live under deep water,
All of us, beasts and men.

—Walter de la Mare

"Three!" I screamed. My parents and I clamped our noses, closed our eyes. The placid pool took us feet first, muffling sound. We walked in slow motion to meet underneath. Drudgery of limbs splitting water. Brilliance of plunging sunbeams. And all the while our bodies tried to rise, lungs ballooned with a burning to breathe, the fat of the flesh inclined toward the sky.

Here's why I'd cried till my parents obliged: it was Saturday, summer. I was sad for reasons I can't recall. Honeysuckle had exploded overnight. I wanted fun for the rest of my life. I was only ten. So there we were in the depths of the pool to see who could keep from laughing the longest. This was one game I planned to lose. I'd thrash to the surface, choking back happiness lighter than air. I'd howl and sputter above my parents. They'd bubble on the bottom, as dour as bass.

But it never came to pass. Sure, Father looked plenty funny. A formidable man on dry land, he paled to baby blue, his swim trunks puffed like diapers. And Mother's hair came undone. Strands meandered like seaweed. She swayed and arranged the ballast of her breasts. A terrible translucence bleached their eyes, magnified by liquid distance. It hurt to see their big bodies flail, wrestling with pressure, using up oxygen, running out of time.

In memory though, we stay languid below. The sky above the pool grows dark, the water black. But me and Mom and Dad adapt, like luminous fish in the dregs of the sea who exude the light by which they live. Our protruding cheeks glow pink with blood. Our brown eyes shine with obdurance. Without a trace of amusement or remorse, our faces are bold from far away, like clock dials lit in the dead of night.

The Hurricane Ride

In salt air and bright light, I watched my aunt revolve. Centrifugal force pressed her ample flesh against a padded wall. She screamed as the floor dropped slowly away, lipstick staining her teeth. But she stuck to the wall as if charged with static and, along with others, didn't fall. She was dressed in checks and dangling shoes, her black handbag clinging to her hip. The Hurricane Ride gathered speed. My aunt was hurtling, blurred. Her mouth became a long dark line. Her delirious eyes were multiplied. Checks and flesh turned diaphanous, her plump arms, gartered thighs. Her face dissolved, a trace of rouge.

I swore I saw through her for the rest of the day, despite her bulk and constant chatter, to the sea heaving beyond the boardwalk, tide absconding with the sand, waves cooling the last of light. Even as we left, I saw the clam-shell ticket stand, the ornate seahorse gate, through the vast glass of my aunt.

When does speed exceed the ability of our eyes to arrest and believe? If the axial rotation of earth is 1,038 miles per hour, why does our planet look languid from space, as bejeweled as my aunt's favorite brooch? Photographs of our galaxy, careening through the universe at over a million miles per hour, aren't even as blurred as the local bus.

Momentum. Inertia. Gravity. Numbers and theories barrel beyond me. It's clear that people disappear, and things, and thoughts. Earth. Aunt. Hurricane. Those words were written with the wish to keep them still. But they travel toward you at the speed of light. They are on the verge of vanishing.

Que Será Será

Cinderella spent a good part of her life impatiently waiting, scooping up cinders that made her sneeze, scrubbing the floor and warbling for her prince. Rip Van Winkle waited too. But groggy, unconscious, his waiting was more like languishing.

Sometimes people accuse other people of living in a dream or a fairy tale, suggesting that they wake up and experience the Now. How officiously they enunciate Now, like Big Ben chiming in London. As if Now were the most obvious source of knowledge, an information kiosk in an airport lobby full of transients. As if Now were the only reliable refuge, a fully equipped modern home in a suburb of quicksand. But Now is a tenuous tightrope between history-future and history-past, and some people have club feet. There is little of interest here anyway: the humming of one's own blood, five measly senses, a certain cast of light. Do you ever say, "I wish it was now"? No. You wish it was an hour from now, or years ago. A fortune teller has no interest in predicting your Now. A psychiatrist is not paid to delve into your Now.

This is not to say that I exclusively love the state of waiting. Projections and delayed gratification are difficult, like drowning in a raindrop. Nor am I necessarily a nostalgic guy, though I plunder the playhouse of my past weekly in the name of art, and it's sad to see the little lamps dim the older I get. And I'm not exactly proud to admit that the things I wait for are largely impossible, like a lavishly landscaped backyard with an Olympic-sized swimming pool, or the envy and respect of my ruthless and famous former classmates. (Are these wishes I wait for lyrical enough? I'm patiently working, polishing phrases on chapped knees, sweeping dirty words under the rug, singing the only song I know.)

Mrs. MacPhee, my piano teacher, loved to sing popular songs. Once, when I asked her, out of the blue, what she would do if she knew the world would end tomorrow, she replied that she'd sing and wait. And then she began a chorus of "Que Será Será" to prove that her voice was worthy of carrying the last sound waves to assail the human ear in the twilight hour of civilization. We gazed out the picture window, and her voice, a rendering of off-key and wildly vibrato notes, was plaintive, hypnotic, and the dusty lamplight seemed to dim, and beyond the towering silhouettes of telephone poles, the red sunset was a conflagration because it was the last sunset before the world was wrecked forever, and I thought, this is not a story, this is not a dream, it could happen now, now, now . . .

Sudden Extinction

The vertebrae of dinosaurs, found in countless excavations, are dusted and rinsed and cataloged. We guess and guess at their huge habits as we gaze at the fossils which capture their absence, sprawling three-toed indentations, the shadowy lattice of ribs. Their skulls are a slight embarrassment, snug even for a head full of blunt wants and backward motives. The Brachiosaurus's brain, for example, sat atop his tapered neck like a minuscule flame on a mammoth candle.

My favorite is Triceratops, his face a hideous Rorschach blot of broad bone and blue hide. The Museum of Natural History owns a replica that doesn't do him justice. One front foot is poised in the air like an elephant sedated for a sideshow. And the nasal horn for shredding aggressors is as dull and mundane as a hook for a hat.

One prominent paleontologist believes that during an instantaneous ice age, glaciers encased these monsters mid-meal —Stegosaurus, Podokesaurus, Iguanadon—all trapped forever like spectrums in glass. But suppose extinction was a matter of choice, and they just didn't want to stand up any longer, like drunk guests at a party's end who pass out in the dark den. There are guys at my gym whose latissimus dorsi, having spread like thunderheads, cause them to inch through an ordinary door; might the dinosauria have grown too big of their own volition?

Derek speaks in expletives and swears that one day his back will be as big as a condominium. Mike's muscles, marbled with veins, perspire from ferocious motion, the taut skin about to split. When Bill does a bench press, the barbell bends from fifty-pound plates; his cheeks expand and expel great gusts of spittle and air till his face and eyes are flushed with blood and his elbows quiver, the weight sways, and someone runs over and hovers above him roaring for one more repetition.

Once, I imagined our exercise through X-ray eyes. Our skeletons gaped at their own reflection. Empty eyes, like apertures, opened onto an afterlife. Lightning-bright spines flashed from sacrums. Phalanges of hands were splayed in surprise. Bones were glowing everywhere, years scoured down to marrow, flesh redressed with white.

And I knew our remains were meant to keep like secrets under the earth. And I knew one day we would topple like monuments, stirring up clouds of dust. And I almost heard the dirge of our perishing, thud after thud after thud, our last titanic exhalations loud and labored and low.

Ark

The zoo is best in the dead of summer when the air is polluted, apocalyptic. Sweltering animals defecate while groups of humans scatter and gasp. This is the season when an elephant's eyes are small black beads of malice. A Bengal tiger lolls on cement, barely blinking, panting and panting, bombarded by popcorn, twitching a little. The orangutans are slow and morose, weary of tires twirling on strings, out of antics at last. Even obtrusive emerald flys stay paralyzed in the shadows. Imagine an inverse of Noah's Ark loaded with languishing animals, capsized in the middle of the city, crammed with trams and baby strollers, not a drop of rain in sight.

The more miserable wildlife becomes, the more we adore those photographs of animals posed like species of people: a chihuahua swami in a tiny turban; a parakeet clad in an ascot and vest; a kitten in a strapless dress. I used to love to manipulate my pet, a collie whose proud countenance could be made to resemble the drooping eyes and tortured hairdos of my relatives and friends.

Today I rejoice whenever I hear that another rare creature has been discovered; the pale, lacy Rotifera that bubbled up from an underwater cave; the small, silent, nocturnal wasp which pollinates Malaysian orchids; the mastodon dry as a piece of beef jerky who thawed from a frozen fjord.

Don't laugh, but just this morning the archaic theory of "spontaneous generation" seemed plausible to me. It was easy to imagine—a storm was building; the light and timbre of wind were right—a snake spawned by a fallen branch, a mouse transmuted from a common rock. I stood in my robe and looked out the window while rain came and changed the earth. Creatures appeared in the clouds and trees, absurd, sublime, thriving, hiding, an arkful of figments, no two alike.

Say "Cheese"

Photography was invented in 1839 and no one suspected that so few decades later Western, Eastern, and Third World nations, when seen from watchful satellites, would be phosphorescent with bursting flashbulbs, the fumes of emulsion tainting the sky. Even the Sufi about to walk over hot coals has arranged for a documentary snapshot and wears his brightest saffron. Even the king of Samoa, in a soft palace of grasscloth, laughs into a viewfinder as his five wives, reflected upside down, cross their ten brown eyes.

And this is not to mention billions of seminal events frozen in eight-by-ten fragments—the births and graduations and weddings whose accumulation fill wallets and albums and shoe boxes, which themselves fill pockets and drawers and closets, which weigh down the peoples and habitats of earth.

Perhaps photography is the cockroach of art forms, obdurate, common, multiplying, destined to outlive us and inherit the future. What picture of the future will, in fact, develop out of the chemical bath of the present?

Here comes the future, hazy at first, a pall that turns into photogenic sunshine, the scene becoming pastoral. A blanket of grass has covered every inch of the past. And so, for the sake of preserving tradition, nomads lug threadbare bags bulging with heirloom photographs. For the most part these photos feature views from airplanes and promontories: oceans, geysers, fountains, statues, obelisks, towers, tombs. And of course portraits, an intricate lineage of relatives who become, receding through the ages, total strangers of mysterious ethnic origins posed in hilarious clothes during obscure rituals often involving extinct animals and unidentifiable implements.

This is a cosmos of startled pink eyes, heads blurred in embarrassment, hands thrust up in protestation, double exposures, headless torsos, inexplicable spots. In one awful shot, a black wall surges in from the margin (half the negative never touched the light) and barrels toward someone's distant cousin. About to be engulfed by oblivion, by a blankness so swift it can't be recorded, by a void so profound it can't be envisioned, having patted stray hair as a last affirmation, you stiffened up and muttered, "Cheese."

....

Futurism

The world's magnificence has
been enriched by a new beauty:
the beauty of speed.

—Fillipo Marinetti,
   futurist artist (1876–1944)

He'd appreciate the names of today's mobile homes: Road Rocket, Dynamo, Fly by Nite. His manifesto would praise the way they monopolize the highway, swaying as though the horizon played music, their contours plump with purpose. He'd describe the decals from various states, and the brightly colored license plates that are pounded into being by anonymous convicts. Those sudden, pungent plumes of exhaust would remind him that people are lost to velocity.

What would happen in his mobile home? The browning of meat, the lathering of hands, the nightly retreat into dreams. But he'd be in motion all the time, his blood careening with greater abandon, his bones honed by minute vibrations, the pop of pistons synchronized with the popping of thoughts into Marinetti's brain.

He grips the wheel, grinds his teeth, accelerates his habitat. He loves the unrolling bolt of the blacktop, buildings quaking in the rearview mirror, red clouds smeared across the sky. You who imagine you're safe in the crosswalk—better look both ways. Marinetti is hard on the horn, laughing as historic landmarks blur by, mad to feel the future arrive, seconds smacking his windshield like insects.

....

Auld Lang Syne

At the stroke of five, secretaries, executives, brokers and clerks fling open windows, gather on roofs, casting into the evening air paper torn from memo pads, a makeshift confetti strewn with messages. Computations, lists, reminders sift through shafts of dying light, past windows reflecting white fragments slowly floating toward bottlenecked traffic, toward startled passersby, everyone speechless, looking up, telephone numbers grazing faces, tentative lunch dates landing on shoulders, name after name falling underfoot. All of this inconsequence, this blizzard of unburdening, is spun by updrafts, cascading off awnings, drifting down for a solid hour.

It's the last day of a long year, and though you've listened to "Auld Lang Syne" a hundred times, you're suddenly moved because the lyrics say that life is a vapor of vanishing attachments. Under the earth or on the earth, friends eventually turn into strangers. And this is only one example where some cliché peels away to reveal a kernel of real feeling. Take those portraits of sallow children with oversized eyes; ludicrous until you notice the ugly hunger in their pitch-black pupils. No wonder Rimbaud loved to read cheap novels; we are busy on every page with banality, reaching for the stars, sinking lower than low, happy as clams, crying rivers, naked as the day we were born.

A lingering pedestrian brushes away a stray notation. Piles of trivia clog the gutter, clutter the crosswalk. Below the quiet street, pipes surge with waste and water, cables coil into the soil, voltage shoots toward buttons and bulbs. Deep beneath the financial district, bits of bone drift through the planet like lightless confetti, years indistinguishable one from another.

Magma burns at the center of the earth. In my first dream of the new year, I'm stoking that fire along with others. Drenched in sweat, we shovel endless heaps of paper into the heat. We watch the licks of fire catch. This is fuel to turn the world: Pick up laundry, Call Louise, Meet with Dan. Tons of memoranda roar up in a gust that warps the scarce air. Ashes fall. Cinders fly. Ink is boldly aglow for a moment, as though our routines were written in flame.

THE END
OF MANNERS

Temple of the
Holy Ghost

Mother was right about the Visible Man. He was meant to be assembled by an older boy. Or at least another boy of ten who wouldn't lose patience inserting the brain, pinning the lungs like wings in the chest, finding a place to fit the heart. It was just too much—dozens of delicate plastic bones, muscles with numbers. I jammed them into his see-through skin. Tiny eyes rolled around in the torso. His bladder rattled. I spent the night transfixed by that miniature physique, the impassive, moonlit features of the face, the rubble of his viscera. I braced myself against the bed and didn't want to be in a body, even a young one.

That was over twenty years ago. But Mother was right, may she rest in peace. Sometimes I stand before the bathroom mirror (behind which lie tablets and salves and syrups) and my skin begins to disappear, and there hover the twin caverns of my troublesome sinus, the coral of my frontal lobe, backsides of astonished eyes, and I say my name and want to be contained within that exhalation, traveling up the esophagus, escaping out of my own mouth, disembodied at last, a pronunciation, a vibration rising in the room, and assuming, everywhere, the shape of air.

···

Leaving

The statistical family stands in a textbook, graphic and un-abashed. The father, tallest, squarest, has impressive shoulders for a stick figure. The mother, slighter, rounder, wears a simple triangle, a skirt she might have sewn herself.

A proud couple of generalizations, their children average 2.5 in number. One boy and one girl, inked in the indelible stance of the parents, hold each other's iconic little hands. But the .5 child is isolated, half a figure, balanced on one leg, one hand ex-tended as if to touch the known world for the last time, leaving probable pounds of bread and gallons of water behind, leaving the norms of income behind, leaving behind the likelihood of marriage (with its orgasms estimated in the thousands), leaving tight margins, long columns, leaving a million particulars, with-out hesitation, without regret.

Spontaneous Combustion

The fireman stands in the center of the stage and waits for applause to die down. An ocean of school children stare at his outfit. His eyes shine like embers beneath his hat. His portentous pause erupts with one word. The vowel of *fire* rises in the room. The children seem to huddle around it, wide-eyed, smelling smoke. Even the teachers grow uneasy, begin to cough and fan themselves.

He names the three components of combustion, heat and air and matter, says their fusion is sometimes spontaneous, off in a corner when no one is awake, brought about by a misplaced match. That dark possibility is now in flames. He names some other common culprits: untended skillets, malfunctioning heaters, smouldering cigarettes. Verging on the incendiary, the children's homes will never seem the same. Fluffy carpets will feed the flames. Every niche is liable to catch. "Be wise," he advises. "Prepare for escape."

. . . .

For weeks after, in the same suburb, the children study their houses for an out. They count the doors, count the windows, compare the width of their shoulders to vents. So fierce is their investigation, so burning their desire for a world beyond the walls, they actually tally cracks in the plaster.

For weeks after, winter descends. Consider the bird's-eye view: moonlit drifts of snow, an expanse of shingle roofs as far as the horizon. Beneath each, small sleepers are fevered with a similar dream; flints click like castanets. White-hot sparks are born. Some survive as full-fledged flames, licking the hems of pajamas. And the children hold their breath. The children spread their arms. The wise children leap from ledges, disappear into another life, into cool cerulean blue.

....

Saturday Night

Can Mother muster enough thrust to leave the earth in a sudden leap? Does Father need words of encouragement, a rabbit's foot, a running start? Will they rise above our suburb at dusk and see it studded with lights? Wind must play havoc with mother's dress, her stole blown back like a vapor trail. Father's suit, diminishing, dark, will become part of the night. What instinct helps them scout for the house, find the right street, land on their feet? How do they breathe, cleaving the air with such soft hats? At the house of the host, can you hear the hail of guests on the roof, the garage, the grass, come eager to mingle, smoke, and tell jokes? Over a cover of cold clouds, bearing bouquets, bottles of wine, decks of cards and dominoes, a sparse arc of punctual people migrate behind the horizon. While aloft like a league of ghosts or gods, does their vision slip through thick ceilings? Can they watch us mimic their kisses, embrace our own backs, burrow hands beneath our bedclothes? Spying their children aglow on earth with a meager heat, do flying parents cry like geese?

The Theory
of Relativity

It's odd how children move through their childhood with such big heads, heads that mature before their bodies. Their nearly finished skulls stare out at the inexplicable world, while the torsos beneath flail and disport themselves trying to grow up. This explains the cuisine consisting of mythical spinach, enriched bread, bottles of milk fortified with hormones and megavitamins. Eat and be like your father, says Mother. Eat and be like me, says Father. The oblong table is a ticket to a greater world, a world where the colossal bodies of adults are like sphinxes moving through the room. Look, their Easter Island heads have broken through the ceiling. Their admonitions about the future are bursting down like thunder.

The world of our fathers is getting too big, much too big. The strained molecules can not contain it. The seams of nuclei begin to burst. Watch out! All the big people are about to explode— the mammoth men with names like Rod, Burke, Deek, names that churn like machinery, and the giant women with clouds for hair and hills for hips and . . . Bang! Boom! The end of an era.

When the dust settles and the coughing subsides and the spinach-covered rubble is cleared away, authority no longer hovers above us. But there are always, always worlds within worlds, and within this new world controlled by us kids with big heads, there exists a microcosmic realm of gnomes and Munchkins and Lilliputians. Yet we are disturbed by the possibility that, for those creatures too, worlds are embedded within their world, worlds for which they are somehow responsible (with this conception, childhood ends). And so we begin to imagine, on a steadily shrinking scale, demi-Lilliputians, and semi-demi-Lilliputians, and so forth until we bawl like babies, clutching at the very last grains of being, which suddenly scatter to the random winds.

....

Aphorism

1

Swine are paralyzed in a pen, their ears pointing toward pearls in the mud. They know these aren't stones or kernels of corn. They know this isn't dew, or some variation of dew. Shudders of incomprehension move through porcine brains. The heat of suspicion slides down their spines, concentric tails tensing. Their big heads begin to bob. Each swine grinds its forty-four teeth. Each pair of eyes grows wide and white.

2

The oysters seem to gape in disbelief; pearls like exclamations sit on the tips of their tongues. Somehow hogs have descended several fathoms, rooting through seaweed and shafts of light, stirring silt from the bottom. They blink against a storm of sardines, bristles rippling on flat flanks. Jets of bubbles fly out from their snouts, causing the baffled oysters to tremble. Whoosh! The shells clamp closed like minds.

The End of Manners

Etiquette columnist Emily Post teeters on the ledge of her New York brownstone. She wears a navy blue dress with white dots, the Peter Pan collar impeccably starched. When she jumps, polka dots drop like rain. While she falls, all around her, from high-rise apartments, arms extend out open windows, feeling for the weather. Blocked by bricks, the humid sky can barely be glimpsed, but it seems to be encroaching. People forget propriety, shed some clothes, wait for the steam to unseal the sky. Wilting, immodest men and women stare down into the street. Their sense of gravity gains momentum the moment before the downpour.

Meanwhile, across the continent, a boy sent to bed for playing with his food dreams he escapes the land of manners. He's lifted from the dinner table toward the ceiling by some mysterious force. His napkin falls like a molted feather. His parents catch it, crane their necks, try to entice him down with pot roast. Their bodies grow tiny, attenuated. Their feeble entreaties precipitate his tears. They fall and snuff the candles. "Sorry," he yells, garbled. His mouth is still full of masticated peas, the thought of which suddenly pleases him. No more the mandatory "May I," the folded hands, the Thank You notes. He'll eat with his fingers, never bathe or behave. Rebel joy, loud as a fly, escalates within him. Higher and higher. He owns the air.

....

THE HOUSE
OF THE FUTURE

A Reminiscence

*Each of my buildings
is a further step
in my search for clarity.*

—Mies van der Rohe

The House of the Future

I was twelve when I saw the House of the Future. It was past the gate to Tomorrowland, commissioned by Walt Disney and molded from Monsanto plastic. Composed of four modular wings cantilevered from a pedestal, all the walls gently curved. The entire structure appeared to hover, weightless and white, more of a craft than a habitat. Shaded by its massive shadow, my parents and I waited in line, impatient for our tour through. Mother was dressed in her Mondrian muumuu, a few big blocks of primary color, father in his Hawaiian shirt, a snarl of palm fronds and stalks of bamboo. I wore mouse ears and madras shorts. "Can you imagine?" Mother exclaimed, craning her neck. Father nudged me, "Suppose this was home."

Hour after hour of my life had been spent in just such supposition. I was a boy obsessed with the future, searching through my comic books for tomorrow's uncanny manifestations: cars humming above the earth, equipped with antigravity engines; supermarkets stocked with hydroponic produce, string beans hefty as baseball bats, pea pods huge as canoes; cryogenics commonplace, the dead suspended in beds of ice to thrive again when science permits. Time was a road that led to utopia— or so I believed—and life, prolonged, would be nearly perfect, humankind molded like plastic till virtue and peace and pleasure prevailed. On the pages of my comic books, all the astonishment promised by the future was evident in architecture: amphitheaters beneath glass domes, arcades on the tiers of ziggurats, conical towers piercing the clouds and bridged by walkways in tubes. Efficient, ideal, inevitable, the buildings of the future would look like machines.

And here was one before me, above me. A prototype of tomorrow, today. Optimism's carapace. A fantastic fragment snatched from the future. "Welcome home," proclaimed the free brochure. "It's always Open House . . . at the House of the Future."

I had been to Open Houses before while riding my bike through our suburb, a flat expanse of single-family dwellings, palm trees, and phone poles lining the streets. I managed to slip past real-estate agents and investigate the houses of strangers, amazed by the foreign furniture, inhaling the odor of other lives. Parting curtains, peeking in drawers, I pretended I was invisible, haunting rooms and haunted by them. Rooms, like colors, were ineffable, of infinite variety, each with its singular evocation.

Again and again, I rummaged through the hall closet till I found the blueprint of my family's house. I unrolled it on the living-room rug, peered down into that mosaic of spaces, feeling as though I were flying. How diminutive were our lives from the sky, the rectangular rooms where we ate or slept, the arcs of our doors pivoting on hinges.

The cruciform floor plan of the House of the Future—three bedrooms, two baths—had this caption beneath: "The winged design of your new home assures full daylight for every room. There are ten times as many windows as you'll find in any ordinary house! And with Thermopane glazing with plastic interlayer, you won't sacrifice safety or comfort!" Our own windows were obscured by drapes—maroon, ochre, cobalt blue—which barely admitted light. What lit our dim house was the ember of mother's cigarette floating back and forth through space as she brooded over my brother. For a year he had languished, reading in his room, one by one his white cells snuffed. Add to this absence of natural light my father's face at evening's end when he'd close the door to my brother's room, his jaw clenched and dark with stubble. But even in the dead of night the House of the Future could simulate day with "Floor to ceiling columns of light / Trans-ceiling polarized panels / Mobile lighting to bathe each room in a glow as warm as the sun."

In the polluted light of southern California, our Spanish house seemed to cling to the earth, the front door aloof in an archway, chunks in the stucco casting shadows. My father spent weekends tending our yard, lugging a hose, hacking at branches, mowing one small patch of grass till his khaki work shirt was soaked with sweat. He believed that gardening hard might help him sleep the whole night through. At noon he'd wail for a glass of seltzer and the neighborhood dogs would start to bark. I'd bring him a tumbler chiming with ice. He'd hold the drink before his face and watch the trails of effervescence before he drained the glass in one gulp. "God," he'd gasp, as though in prayer, handing back the glass.

One Sunday he purchased a plaster fawn and stuck it next to the sign that read "Casa de Cooper." He sat on the steps and stared at that fawn, and the fawn stared back till the sun descended. My mother and I joined him in the twilight. "Almost lifelike," Mother observed. Then we turned our backs on a few weak stars and filed through the door to dinner.

Inching closer to the House of the Future, my parents were using their brochures as fans while I pored over its pages. The copy was long on promises. One blurb boasted "Enter the 'Atoms for Living' kitchen, where cooking is controlled, carefree—and automatic all the way!" I wanted for my mother a kitchen of this kind, with its ultrasonic counter cleaner "pre-programmed to work when the wife is away," its recyclable plastic cups and plates which were melted down and re-vacuformed so no dish ever need be washed. As it was, Mother spent every spare minute in her kitchen, a Lucky burning at the edge of the sink while she labored over meals for my brother: red wedges of watermelon, precisely bite-sized, seeds extracted; gems of oil on the surface of soup, a chicken broth with carrots and onions. A devotee of convenience foods, I begged my mother to stock her Frigidaire with cardboard cylinders of premade dough, tubs of Sta-Fluff whipped cream, one-minute oats and instant Jello, icy entrees in tinfoil trays, dormant until they reached the heat. I preferred items with preservatives like polysorbate and BHT; they had a shelf life of several years, stayed fragrant and moist against all odds, and offered a taste of eternity.

It was the permanence, the durability of plastic that made the

Monsanto house a marvel. The wings, it was said, would never sag. The plastic floor would never buckle, chip or crack. The custom-made furnishings—melamine polymer tables, vinyl-dipped chairs, urethane couches, polyester pillows—were virtually indestructible. "Open your door," urged the brochure, "to the wonders of modern materials." I relished the names of Monsanto products: Polyflex . . . Resinox . . . Resimine . . . Scriptite . . . Stymar . . . Lauxite . . . Ultron . . . Lytron—a chant that compelled the next century closer. "In fact," proclaimed one boldface caption, "it could be said that hardly a natural material occurs in its original state anywhere in your new home!"

By twelve I had developed a disregard for nature. I was mesmerized by office lobbies, the enameled ports of filling stations, the chrome appointments in coffee shops. Nature was the force to which my brother was forsaken; it consumed his pale body like soap, stripping him of flesh and motion. Steel and glass and concrete and chrome: I thought of these words with reverence, like words used in a manifesto. My zeal for modernity found confirmation in a book from my junior high school library entitled *20th Century Architecture*. One glance at the chapter on Mies van der Rohe led me to see him as a spiritual ally. Dear Mies, I might have written, The big airy skeletons of your skyscrapers are so sturdy, and your skins of glass so clear, there seems to be no building there and finally the light of the sky can burn through.

One could look down through the plexiglass steps to the House of the Future and glimpse a large reflecting pool, shivering and shaped like an amoeba. It bore little resemblance to the rubber pools, rowdy children wading within, which dotted our local yards. It was in a pool like one of these, riddled with leaves and drowning bees, that my brother, Gary, learned to swim. In the summer months before illness struck, Gary acquired a driver's license, bought a Thunderbird convertible on time, and advertised in the *Bel Air News*, "Give a call to Gary Cooper, swimming instructor to the children of the stars."

My mother tried to hide her excitement when the secretaries of Paul Newman, Tony Curtis, and Karl Malden phoned our house. She suggested that Gary take me with him so that I might meet these celebrities, mingle with their offspring and (this part was our secret agreement) tell her facts about their homes and habits that even a prying reporter couldn't discover.

That sweltering day is tempered in my memory by pool after cool pool. Set like jewels in expansive estates, they came in every shape: oval, kidney, rectangle, round. In pool houses aromatic with cocoa butter, terry-cloth towels and latex bathing caps, my brother and I changed into our trunks. Each dressing room contained some tropical touch: a full-length mirror festooned with fishnet, a mussel shell that doubled as a soap dish, a brittle blowfish hanging from the ceiling. Dean Martin's pool house was emblazoned with the sign "We don't swim in your toilet—Please don't pee in our pool."

Most of that distant afternoon—a dozen particulars of privacy and privilege—is blurred by bright sunlight, hairpin turns on canyon roads, the parting of electric gates. What I remembered to tell my mother was how Gary stopped at the top of Bel Air and stared at the city below, his shoulders tan, zinc on his nose, making plans for notoriety and a mansion filled with music and maids.

Piped into the House of the Future with purified air and a sweet synthetic scent was futuristic music, a metallic mixture of keyboard and percussion. We could hear it as we neared the door where a docent, like a stewardess, stood in a silver uniform and greeted each guest with the salutation, "So glad you could make it. Welcome aboard." We had finally reached the resin threshold, ready and willing to be transported.

For all his pallor, thinning limbs, veins emerging on the surface of his skin, my brother's eyes continued to shine, avid for news of the future. Gary loved to hear about that house. For weeks he asked me to tell him again of the telephone with a video screen that allowed you to see who was calling, the one-piece, lightweight bathroom sink that adjusted height at the push of a button. While Gary tested spoonfuls of soup, I propped myself on the edge of his bed and replayed the tour over and over, my memory sharp as a phonograph needle. And he'd always interrupt with the question, "Did it look like a giant four-leaf clover?" and always I'd answer, "That's exactly it." What was luck to my brown-eyed brother during the last of his life but stories of a hovering house, a harbinger, the prospective shape of plastic.

The Monsanto Chemical Company envisioned instant communities, the modular units mass produced, designed to stack on delivery trucks. The brochure had stressed the advantages of living in a shelter of changeable parts: "The house adapts to every situation. Family growing? Simply order more wings in the color of your choice! Dismantle the wings you no longer need as soon as the kids move on!" It was assumed the public of tomorrow would be in a constant state of flux, that "wing lots" would be as common as car lots, selling modules new and used. A mobile world was easy to imagine. Born of an urgent need for speed, Texaco stations appeared on corners, trailer parks claimed the hills. New freeways cut across our city, overpasses unfurling in air, onramps swooping up from the street, five-lane highways crowded with cars, their tail fins fashioned for flight.

Father drove a Plymouth Deluxe and sat like a pilot behind the wheel. He changed lanes as though pursued and scowled at the drivers he overtook. When Father was forced to stop at a light, he'd check his watch and tap the dash, wanting nothing more than to be in motion. That mammoth car rumbled with thrust, a machine greedy for premium gas. The interior was ample and grand. The plush seats, brushed velour, seemed to extend in perspective forever. I'd sit in the back with my cheek against the glass and count the cars we'd pass, noting their color, mouthing their make: Valiant, Rambler, Triumph, Dodge. Sometimes their fronts looked like a face, and I'd try to place their disposition. The Lincoln Continental, for instance, expressed an impatience as great as my father's, with its headlights on the diagonal, its grill like gritted teeth. Whisked to the drugstore or nursery or market, we missed collision by a coat of paint. One day we left my brother with his nurse and drove our Plymouth into the desert. Dad scanned for real estate, for raw resources. He lived a life of reckless speculation, guessing what could be rendered from what, his future always in the making. A mirage of water preceded us like hearsay. I leaned my weight against the front seat, gazed out toward the curve of the earth, and like a muse above Father's shoulder, whispered "faster" into his ear.

My father loved progress in all of its forms, velocity on the open road, schemes that promised he'd get rich quick. The future was like a vehicle that my father could commandeer. And Mother, in her superstitious way, believed she too could control the future. She based decisions on a lucky number and behaved according to her horoscope. She even considered changing Gary's name, believing that might change his fate.

I pictured the progress of my brother's disease as a gathering of dark clouds that closed off any avenue of light, clusters of heavy, tentative drops, a downpour held in suspension for a year. Below it stood our stucco house, my parents wishful within its walls, Father postdating payments on our car, mother blowing ghostly smoke.

It rained the evening my brother died. As we drove home from the hospital, another city was reflected in the pavement, its palm trees smeared, its marquees incoherent, its upturned towers sunk in puddles. Father drove the Plymouth slowly, apologizing for every wrong turn. Mother slumped in the front seat, sedated with a dose of Miltown, unable to lift her cigarette, softly asking "Where's my son? Swimming with the stars?" With my cheek pressed against the glass—cold comfort—I was somewhere far in the future, walking into buildings where the climate was controlled, wending my way through lobbies and halls. Dear Mies, I was thinking, I love how your skyscrapers shimmer like prisms, rising up from the surface of the cities, story after perfect story overshadowing everything on earth.

Dream House

My mother and father and brother were asleep. It was quiet except for the ticks and groans of our Spanish house contracting in the cold. Degree by degree the temperature had dropped; November deepened. Undertones of orange were gone from the sky, the threat of rain sustained for weeks. What was to come was held in suspension, waited to happen: the blast of pain in my brother's chest, sensation drained from his fingers and toes, the blood in his body freed from its boundaries, leaving his lips, the ambulance attendants surging through our door, strangers in white who flanked a gurney, my father begging them not to use the siren—whatever you do, don't use that siren—afraid the sound would frighten his son.

But none of this had happened yet. It was just after dawn. A pale light filled the hall. I stood in the doorway and stared at my parents sprawled in sleep. Their limbs were flung at improbable angles. Their mouths were slack. Beneath closed lids, eyes followed the course of dreams whose theme I tried to guess. But their faces—sunken in a stack of pillows, released from the tension of fear and hope—were emptied of all expression.

Nailed on the door to my brother's room was a road sign he'd stolen from Coldwater Canyon: NOT A THROUGH STREET. At the age of seventeen, Gary had been diagnosed by grayhaired Dr. Wertz. Since then his room had remained the same. A cork bulletin board was covered with snapshots of my brother posed at poolside with various stars, as tall as them, as tan. On his end table were amber bottles, vials of pills, each imprinted with the time, method and amount to take. For a night light, my brother had recovered from a closet his childhood lamp in the shape of Saturn, its rings casting a mammoth shadow around the ceiling's perimeter. The blanket Gary lay beneath matched a padded headboard. The print contained a white house, a green tree, a red car. These were repeated over and over, the net effect a crowded town. It was odd to see my brother's head—sweat beading above his brow, scalp showing through sparse hair— set in such simple, redundant surroundings.

I wandered in, sat by his bed, and watched him sleep. He didn't stir. No evidence of dreaming on his gaunt, impassive features. Where, I wondered, did my brother's soul go when it wasn't alert in his eyes? I squeezed his hand till his eyelids lifted back. My brother slowly surfaced from sleep, tasting his mouth, testing his fingers, reclaiming his body, becoming himself. He started to speak . . . was gone again. All that remained was the heat of his fever vibrant in the air between us.

Next thing I knew I was in a pool. Waves around me were brimming and breaking. I was trying to part the weight of the water. I paddled into my brother's arms. But then he'd let go, move away, and I'd tread toward him again. Rivulets ran down the slope of his shoulders. His neck was corded with moving muscle. Wet hair clung to the nape of his neck. The scent of his skin was incentive to swim, sweeter, magnified, more distinct every time I struggled close. And then I awoke, still sitting in his chair. Gary, bewildered, was standing before me, floating in a blue bathrobe which hadn't fit him for months.

"Bernard," he asked, "what are you doing?"

All I could say was, "Learning to swim."

Each morning my family converged in the kitchen, and though our dreams were over for the day, if any place could prolong the fantastic logic of dreams, our cluttered kitchen was it. The ceramic teapot was a southern belle, her right arm the spout, her left the handle. The bottle opener was shaped like the state of Michigan, Coca-Cola tops wrenched off in the hollow spot of Lake Superior. The salt and pepper shakers were a pair of pleasure craft, the seasonings visible through tiny port-holes. "Ahoy," my father would mumble, sprinkling salt on his poached egg.

Since the onset of Gary's illness, my mother had purchased household objects which looked like something other than what they were. She searched the sundries section of the local Wool-worth's or ordered them from one of the myriad ads in the back of *House and Garden* magazine. The offerings in those ads were often the topic of early morning talk. Crammed into the vinyl seat of the built-in breakfast nook, we listened while my mother, waving one hand for emphasis, read about some re-markable bargain—two oven mitts, say, printed respectively with the faces of John and Jackie Kennedy—passing the photo-graph under our noses in case we needed proof.

I'd search through the magazine for Before and After pic-tures, and point them out to my brother. Together we gawked at Mrs. Orin Potter; on the left she was wizened and dowdy and despondent, but thanks to a regimen of Sleep Tight Night Creme, on the right Mrs. Potter was a woman renewed, her wrinkles vanquished, eyes bright. Or Mike Bono, an under-nourished weakling, his ribs distended, shoulders imploding, who became a bundle of brazen muscle. There were tonics that scared up harvests of hair, salves that caused the bosom to bur-geon, anatomies strapped and wracked to perfection, by hook or by crook, by prosthesis or paint. I wanted those ads to con-vince my brother that people improved, that a sow's ear could become a silk purse, light arise from beneath a bushel, and water turn to wine.

It was Gary who noticed the Dream House contest. Spon-sored by *House and Garden* in conjunction with the architectural firm of Ellsworth & Watley, the ad contained an illustration of Tudor, ranch, and colonial houses situated in a sleeper's head. The contest was open to amateur architects everywhere, one entry per family. Rules stated the medium (a pencil sketch on typewriter paper) as well as the dual criteria—originality and feasibility—used to judge the winners of a five-hundred-dollar cash prize. "The two bedroom, two bath house of your dreams must not exceed one thousand square feet of floorspace. All the rest is up to you! Your imagination is the only limit."

Gary read these rules aloud and our parents retreated into meditation before they began to execute their plan. Mother, I suppose, dreamed of a cavernous pantry. Father was no doubt concocting a garage, as vast and immaculate as any showroom, in which to park his Plymouth. For the second time that morning I stared at my parents, attempting to guess the nature of their dreams. But even the final draft of their dream house did little to clarify the life they desired; they haggled over round rooms, spiral stairs, double doors, and by the time the drawing was complete, it was so smeared with erasures and revisions, it appeared to be more of a natural phenomenon than a building, a gray monsoon or a cumulus cloud tossed about by wind and whim.

Posterity. I didn't know exactly what the word meant, but I sensed it had to do with events of the present viewed in the wiser light of the future, and I remember thinking I should keep that drawing, that its wavering walls and incoherent angles were as accurate a representation of my family's house as I'd ever see, and I knew, even then, that the force which impelled my parents' hands and warped those lines was the same force distorting my brother's body, death and its attendant pressure, pulling at us in every room, ubiquitous as gravity, and nothing my parents could do would stop it, not Mother consulting her horoscope, keeping her yellowed fingers crossed, casting salt behind her back; not Father venturing into the yard, making thrive his patch of grass, training bougainvillea to a trellis, the odor of growth encircling our house.

I conceived of death as dreamless sleep, nothing more. Gary was easing his body into death as he'd eased himself into a pool of cold water, trembling against the shock of submersion, inch by inch until he was under.

There was little discernible difference to me in those days between dreaming and waking; both states shared the same skewed perspectives, the same oblique and leaden light. Irrational events were as likely to occur as ordinary ones. I'd find my mother ironing the same shirt over and over while she smoked and spoke in non sequiturs, veering from neighborhood gossip to the toll of chemotherapy. And sometimes from the window I heard my father talking to himself as he walked to the car, a mumble of comments and nonsense, and he'd have to pat his pockets for his key ring, and he'd have to choose which key he wanted, and he'd have to stop and recollect why. With increasing frequency, my parents became remote beyond retrieval; often they called me by Gary's name, and never once realized their error.

Was I stealing my brother's strength? Was I thick and heavy from mother's meals, or were measures of my brother's health leaving him and melding to me, slapped and bonded like wads of clay on a sculptor's figurine? Gary was dying with a polite silence, an awful obedience, and the more frail my brother became, the more I was seized by restlessness; my bones ached, my hands were cramped, my eyes could not absorb enough. I was up half the night devouring books on architecture while the television and the radio blared. Like Mother's runaway monologues and Father's cryptic muttering, what fueled those architect's manifestos was a strain of combative anguish. "The past be damned," one began. "As if we—the accumulators and generators of movement, with the noise and speed and fervor of our lives—could live in buildings encrusted with a carnival of decoration. The city must be an ideal projection of modern life and spirit! We must construct our houses according to every scientific and technical resource! We must reject everything grotesque, cumbersome, and alien to our progress and vitality!" And as I read on, only half understanding yet nodding my head, light from the television caused the room to flicker like matter in a frantic dream.

Le Corbusier wrote that all architecture was, first and fore-most, a product of light and shadow, the articulation of mass and volume brought about by an interplay between them. On dark November nights, had a passerby glanced at our house, he would have beheld, through a break in the drapes, a living room shimmering cathode blue, an ember-red and smoke-filled kitchen, Saturn glowing in a corner bedroom—the casements, eaves, aging beams, and ripples of a tile roof defined by the light from those windows.

Dog House

Lester and Cora Lavitt were my parents' closest friends. Lester ran a chauffeur service that catered to movie producers, and Cora bred Shetland sheepdogs in their yard. They'd pull into our driveway, idling in a limousine, one of three from their "fleet." Without so much as lifting our heads from our books, my brother and I had learned to tell which Cadillac they were driving by the chorus of its horn: the gold one played a bar of "La Cucaracha," the black one, "We're in the Money," and the longest one, midnight blue, bleated the opening notes to "Hail, Hail, the Gang's All Here." My parents never ceased to find this amusing. They'd run to the front door, laughing and shaking their heads. Then they'd say to Les and Cora, "You crazy kids." Mother and Cora embraced, inhaling each other's perfume ("Delicious! What is it?"), referring to one another as "honey." Les and my father threw left hooks, winced in mock pain, called each other "buddy boy." These endearments never varied, but the inflection changed depending on the seriousness of the topic, the emphasis of syllables capable of conveying a range of emotions from impatience to confidentiality.

A fun couple, as my parents described them over and over, Cora was wall-eyed and husky-voiced, a lover of gimlets and practical jokes, and Lester was an amateur ventriloquist, throw-ing his voice at every opportunity, with only moderate expertise as far as Gary and I were concerned. Some people were fooled, however, and it was not uncommon when we all walked down the street for some bewildered pedestrian to crane his neck toward the top of a high-rise as a small voice threatened to jump. Lester's ventriloquism was looked upon by my parents as a gift, and they requested on numerous occasions that he teach the fine points to me and my brother.

"Go on, Les. They'd love to learn. Wouldn't you, boys?"

Gary and I, having planned this beforehand, responded by saying, "Thank you, no. Indeed we would not," trying not to move our lips.

"That's telling 'em," Cora rasped, chortling hard, her gimlet sloshing out of its glass. "Don't let my hubby make you into dummies."

This exchange became a ritual, its finale involving Lester burying his head in his palms and feigning sobs until we gave in. "Ready?" he'd ask, sitting up, his face still red from hyperventilation. "The problem letters are B, F, M, P, and W. So, for B you say 'Vhee.' Say it—'Vhee.' "

"Vhe-e-e," we'd croon in unison, and my parents and Cora, too. And so it went till we reached the Duggle-U, Lester commending us after each consonant.

During Les and Cora's subsequent visits, we advanced to the practice of tricky words: carpets—*carfets;* bedroom—*vhedroom;* amusing—*ang-yusing.* Finally the six of us were able to conduct conversations composed of the difficult sentences Lester designed to test our proficiency.

"The queen stopped playing the piano," Cora exclaimed, perfectly motionless. In fact, all of us sat stiffly because tensing the rest of our bodies helped us control our lips.

"Now you can cut the cake," Mother enunciated.

"Don't draw the nose," Father warned. "The old lady owns it."

And we'd periodically glance at Lester, who'd say in his thin, distant voice, "Fractice nakes Ferfect."

Although, for me, Lester and Cora's antics quickly grew tedious, my parents thrived in their presence. A man with two voices; a woman who saw double; hours of play and repartee multiplied exponentially. They both admired my mother's taste, delighted by the swizzle sticks topped with tiny starfish, and they never tired of touring our yard, taking clippings from plants at Father's insistence. In the early stages of my brother's illness, Lester and Cora comforted my parents by praising Dr. Wertz. A doll, Cora called him, a miracle worker; the man must use voodoo. There was something receptive, responsive, something fluid about the Lavitts' characters, despite their imposing height and girth. And above all, they possessed a perpetual eagerness to participate in any stunt my parents dreamed up.

One day they arrived with a doghouse tied to the roof of the limo. My father had just bought a Bell and Howell camera for making home movies, and the scenario of his first film involved all of us crawling into that doghouse. Through stop-action photography, each of us would have a moment to crawl out and make room for the next person, but the final effect, my father assured, would set us on our ears. It was decided that we'd enter according to height, me first, then my brother, my parents next, and last the Lavitts. Mother mixed a batch of gimlets while Father secured the camera to the tripod. By the time the equipment and light were right, my mother and Cora were slurring their words.

During the shooting, my father was liberal with phrases such as "Cut," "Print," and "That's a take."

Cora patted her blonde bouffant and applied more lipstick before her "scene," calling my father "Mr. DeMille."

The finished film was seamless and brief, the illusion a huge success. So successful, in fact, that during the preview, I thought I recalled being huddled with my family and the Lavitts in the doghouse, in utter darkness, the odor of pine, vodka, perfume, all of us panting like animals.

There existed in the course of my brother's disease a phase when kindness on the part of friends seemed to him like consolation, or worse, an admission of hopelessness. When Cora gave the dog to Gary, he held it for a few seconds, then handed it to me. He quietly thanked her, returned to his room. "You have the house," Cora said to his back. "I thought you'd like a dog to put in it."

And so the dog became mine by default. I called him Pudgey, an inappropriate name considering how wiry he was, his muzzle brown and narrow, his white legs thin as sticks of chalk. We kept him confined to the kitchen, where he raced in aimless circles, slipping on the linoleum, paws clicking like castanets. With Shetland sheepdogs, Cora had explained, nervousness and loyalty are two outstanding traits. In those respects Pudgey and I were alike: I battled him for a rubber pork chop; I strangled him with hugs.

When my family had gone to the doctor's, I'd make the dog impersonate humans. In a paisley scarf, he looked every bit as anxious as mother, sighing deep sighs, his eyes perplexed. He wouldn't sit still in father's vest, shuddering to shake it away. Pudgey wasn't so much funny as fascinating in those outfits; a beast obeying the laws of propriety, his animal instinct disguised.

My instinct was to kiss my brother. Not a quick, fraternal kiss, but a kiss intent and impassioned. In dreams we'd be immersed in water and I'd gaze at his body unabashed: the wet flesh of his forearms, sinew braided down his back, the shadow cast by his jaw. Shamed awake by the need in those dreams, I told myself— I can't remember just how; I didn't have words for it then—that this must be mourning, a reverie for his vanishing health, close to desire, but not desire. Yet some days it seemed that my every nerve was clenched against an attraction to my brother. The more I found his body compelling and the closer a companion I became, the less I dared to touch him. Instead, nearly every evening, I presented him with my drawings of cities, intricate, hypothetical cities. Hiding my desire became second nature, like learning to speak without moving my lips.

House of Cards

Mine was the spartan room in our home—bed, bureau, chair—a small domain where less was more. But my bureau drawers were stocked with all the games I'd ever owned, most of which I thought I'd outgrown until they served their new purpose: helping my brother slide through time. My mission on Saturday mornings was to plan a day of distraction for Gary. Our recreation took place in my room; Gary's room smelled of the disinfectant mother spread over every surface. We could hear her in there scrubbing and spraying, armed with ammonia, Comet, Lysol. When she passed by my door, we caught the stern expression of a woman who fought an invisible enemy, colonies of bacteria, swarms of spore. The astringent odors arising from his room confirmed for my brother his delicacy; he was prone to harm carried on the air and exuded by the furniture, menaced by all he breathed or touched. Gary must have felt as though he were living in a house of cards, that the merest breath, the wrong move could set in motion a chain reaction which threatened to topple everything solid—the lintels and beams of our stucco house, his own bones.

The instant I sensed my brother's remorse, I'd offer up another activity. A particularly rich source of pastimes was a book entitled "Things for Boys to Do," and though it was meant for younger boys, we indulged ourselves without restraint. Some of the newsprint pages were blank except for numbered dots. They seemed to be scattered at random, a constellation of dark stars. But connected by a pencil in the proper order they'd yield a mitt and baseball bat, a stage coach, tiger, bicycle, frog. We guided our pencils through countless mazes. We searched for objects hidden in pictures, a bowl of lemons in a winter landscape, a jackknife in a bouquet. Once detected, those objects leapt from background to foreground, apparent forever after. Images of Gary did this too, rising at night to the forefront of my thoughts: his face fixed in concentration, his arm grazing mine.

Clue, Monopoly, Chinese checkers, jigsaw puzzles: in four consecutive Saturdays my battery of games had been exhausted and I had to resort to my own invention. I pantomimed the titles of movies while Gary lay on my bed and guessed *The House of Wax* or *Gone with the Wind* after only a few frenetic gestures. I posed riddles, told jokes, did imitations of John Wayne, never allowing a moment to pass without the noise of improvisation. And then there came the Saturday Gary was too weak to join me in my room.

Without my brother to entertain, that afternoon was interminable. Hours were spent in a vigil at my window, watching clouds accumulate, their shadows passing over the grass and a riot of roofs that met the horizon.

At the urging of Dr. Wertz, my parents considered hiring a part-time nurse, Martin Ascerol. Martin was "new," as my mother put it, an emigré from Lebanon. She had to work to suppress her mistrust of anyone Arab. They possessed, she claimed, a natural animosity toward the Jews. The day before his interview, my mother displayed our brass menorah on the sideboard in the dining room. "If he looks at it and doesn't blink, I'll consider him hired." Whether Martin blinked I never knew, but he disarmed my mother with a hesitant charm, weighing his words, hands in his lap. The matter of his employment was settled as soon as he and my mother embarked on a long discussion comparing Arab and Israeli cuisine. Fidgeting in a wing chair, I watched them talk, wary of Martin's black pupils, gold rings, thick beard. Wary, that is, until he asked me at the interview's end, "You are the brother? Tell me what you love."

I had never known anyone to ask questions as broad as Martin's. He asked them in low, probing tones, surprised and pleased by his grasp of the language. To my father returning home from work, "Are the days good or not so good?" To my mother after a phone call to Cora, "Her heart is large?"

Martin came to our house three days a week. What transpired in my brother's room I knew of only by inference; Martin kept the door closed. Standing in the hall, I could sometimes hear a muffled exchange—the lilt of Martin's question, the pause preceding my brother's answer. Though I could never make out the exact nature of these conversations, their hush and infrequency suggested that the topics had little bearing on the outside world, but pertained instead to the immediate realm of Gary's comfort, the warmth of his blanket or ease of his breathing. Martin would pound my brother's back, a hollow percussion. Then the hiss of a respirator. A sponge wrung into a bowl of water. Caps unsnapped. The rattle of tablets. Silence as my brother slept. Of all the noises coming from that room, quiet was the most palpable, a setting for the jewel of my brother's recovery.

There was also the sound of cards being shuffled. Martin, my mother told me, loved to play solitaire, the only card game he knew. Given Martin's deference to my family, his reserves of patience and nurturing, it was fitting that he played a game in which no one else was challenged or defeated. And so, with every slap of the cards, I stood in the hall and thought of Martin, considered his mercy, wondered how he mustered so much for an ailing stranger. My mother had called him "our angel," and I imagined Martin floating through the air as he carried out his duty.

At the age of twelve, I envisioned that which afforded hope in direct opposition to gravity. The burdensome past would sink like lead and the feather-light future ascend. The Monsanto House, Buckminster Fuller's Dymaxion House, Le Corbusier's Villa Savoie, each was supported by slender poles.

The first time my father drove Martin home, it came as no surprise to me that he and his American wife, Anna, lived in a cantilevered house jutting out from the Hollywood hills. "My God," said my father, pulling his Plymouth into a carport suspended above a precipitous slope. The three of us gingerly closed the car doors, leaned against the redwood railing, peered at the succulents hugging the hill and plunging into darkness.

"A question?" Martin asked my father.

Flashlight in hand, Martin led Anna, me, and my father under the house. We followed a path that cut through overgrown bushes. Martin called out the names of obstacles along the way. "A rock," he'd say, "A root." Anna's glasses slipped down her nose. Pushing them back, she lost her balance, wobbled, slid. Martin caught her under the elbows. He led us to a dirt promontory, narrow and flat, held back by a retaining wall. The beam of Martin's flashlight illuminated three immense concrete pylons wedged into the hillside. Secured into each was a metal pillar. The pillars were crisscrossed by metal cables. Martin slid the light to the top of each pillar, lingering on a ring of bolts. Washed by wavering light, the underside of the house, a vast expanse of planks, was exposed to the cold and the night. Anna shivered, hugged her ribs. "If I thought about it," she said, "I'd never get to sleep."

In the wan light, I could see snails climbing the pillars, the gloss of their trails. Spider webs clung to corners. Below us, a startled bird bristled in the bushes and let out a guttural cry. It was as if Martin's house were a rock that someone had suddenly wrenched up, revealing a rut of moist earth teeming with primal life. The faces of Martin, Anna, my father, lit from beneath by the flashlight, looked feral and unfamiliar. Their eyes blinked against the breeze. Puffs of their breath appeared in the air.

As if to assure us that he and Anna were not alone in this tenuous existence, Martin directed the beam of light to houses on either side of his. As far as the eye could see, poles arose from the steep grade; flimsy constructions, like houses of cards, were propped atop them. Walls abutted in mid-air. Balconies dangled from sliding glass doors. The figures of people moved in windows, eating, reading, washing dishes, heedless of the thin slice of floor that spared them from falling into the canyon.

Clambering back to the level of the street, Anna invited us to see the inside of the house on our next visit. My father accepted her offer, but once inside the car he said he wouldn't set foot in that house. The sight of it had unsettled me as well—every building I knew of was underpinned by earth that lay just below a thin skin of asphalt, veined with pipes and telephone wires, pitted with pools of tar and gas, bits of fossil, shards of bone.

House on Fire

The drive home from Martin's was quiet. While careening from lane to lane, my father mulled over his investments. That November alone, he was engaged in the refurbishing of a duplex he'd purchased in Pomona with Lester, escrow on a plot of barren land on the outskirts of Lancaster, the marketing of kosher burritos under the auspices of the Pico Nuevo Hot Sauce Company (he just had to find a rabbi who'd bless them), and the production of an air freshener for the car along with his partner, Rudy Granatelli, brother of the race car driver, Andy Granatelli.

"We'll call it," he had told my mother, "Auto Aroma by Granatelli."

"But won't people think you mean Andy Granatelli?"

"It's Rudy's name too," he'd snapped.

In the back seat of our car, I was swept along in my father's wake; his every project, a proverbial carrot, dangled before the vast windshield. If he was rough with the clutch, if he ignored red lights, if he drove, as he put it, "like a house on fire," he did so because opportunity beckoned.

Both my parents had grown up in the meatpacking district of Chicago, and according to their stories Chicago was not the home of the dazzling skyscrapers I'd read about in books, those Van der Rohe monoliths facing the waterfront, but a tenement city of bricks and stoops, loading docks smeared with the blood of beef, the streets clogged by battalions of carts, by hawkers selling paper shoes, peddlers of pots, grinders of knives, where commerce was chaos seven days a week, its stench and noise assaulting the senses. Only one among their stories offered respite —the story of their first meeting. A mutual friend was abandoning a one-room apartment he rented on South Street—the building had been condemned—and at the farewell party the host, with a bucket of black tempera, painted the shadows of his guests on the wall. Shadows brought my parents together. "Such a figure," my father would say, "right there on the wall. You couldn't have missed her."

They eloped the day my mother turned sixteen—old enough for a driver's license. Yet my mother never applied for one. When I was eight I'd asked her why. She sat me down, held my hand, brushed back strands of her auburn hair. After a moment of silence she said, "You know I was raised in Chicago, right? But I bet you didn't know I was born in Russia. I don't remember Russia, of course; I was two when we left. I swam here on your Grandpa's back. Don't look at me like that. And if I go to the Department of Motor Vehicles, they'll find out I'm not a citizen and deport me in a flash."

I vowed never to betray her secret. I suffered the thought of my mother's absence, was better behaved at the age of eight than I'd been before or since. When my father pleaded with her to take driving lessons, I threw myself between them. "No," I moaned, "don't make her do it. You be the driver, Dad."

Speeding back from Martin's through the neighborhoods of Hollywood, I glimpsed the mansard roofs of France, the dormers of England, the shingled walls of Cape Cod. History and geography had been reinvented by architects, the streets a jumble of places and times. Houses slid by the windows of the car, so bizarre a succession of styles that our route seemed dreamed instead of driven. And soon the windows were dense with steam, the edges of the buildings blurred, seeping into space like stains.

Every time I arrived home, I expected to find my brother well, his pallor replaced by his former tan, his limbs thickened, his energy replenished. The touch of the doorknob ignited in my mind so strong an image of Gary's remission, I fully believed that, thanks to Martin, I'd find him cured. For that entire year, the very act of entering our house was synonymous with hope: the glint of the knob, its pivot in my palm, the burst of heat and light on my face. As I ran down the hall, each instant opened like another door, a door dividing faith from dread.

I'd find Gary bundled in blankets, too hot or too cold. In either case his lips were cracked, his swallowing audible. He expended tremendous effort bending a straw to his mouth. He'd glance at me as if to say: I can do this, but the time it will take will make us both unhappy. I lacked my brother long before he perished. Though he still inhabited our house, though his needs and breathing swelled his room, though he may have been lying across from me, I often drifted into memories.

There is so little to remember of the dying. An angle of their daydreaming face. The time they straightened the collar of your shirt. And what of their words? You retain them in your mind for months, a gem of a joke, a clever quip, an offhand remark with the impact of an adage, but the words erode like the hillsides of the city and no amount of recollection can hold them back.

Once, after a fire marshal had visited my junior high school to lecture the students on safety, I described his film, *Playing with Fire*, to my bedridden brother: an overloaded electrical outlet; burning grease spilled from a skillet; a cigarette igniting a mattress; the sudden combustion of house after house.

"Tell me what we'd do," Gary asked, "if our house was burning down."

"Well . . ." I replied, closing my eyes. But I couldn't picture flames or smoke, couldn't recall the marshal's advice. I imagined our evacuation taking place on an ordinary night. Still, my heart was pounding in alarm. I entered my brother's room as he slept, roused him awake, scooped his medicine into my pocket. I carried Gary toward the door. Where I'd take him I didn't know; what mattered was his body, limp and light in my arms. His weightlessness had a purpose after all—my brother was sleek for a quick escape. "I'm waiting," he said as I opened my eyes.

Bringing Down the House

I struggled with algebraic equations, always at a loss for x. The study of seventh-grade mathematics implied that all problems had solutions, one need only supply the right quotient, puzzle out the proper steps. It would have been impossible, of course, to inform Mr. Morse that I disagreed with algebra on principle, that reason was as fleeting a thing as refractions in a pool of water, and so I bided time in class by drawing buildings in the margins of my notebook. Without a grasp of mathematics, I realized my buildings were doomed to collapse.

Distraught by my grades, seeing my obsession with architecture as distraction rather than destiny, my mother enrolled me in classes at the Meglan Academy for Young Actors. Ever since Gary's trips to Bel Air, Mother subscribed to fan magazines, followed the gossip of movie immortals, walked on Tuesdays to the local matinee, and hoped I'd take an interest in acting. "Just try it," she said. "You might make millions." I stuck out my tongue and rolled my eyes. "See," she said, "you're a natural."

The Meglan Academy was housed in an enclave of bungalows a block west of Vine on Hollywood Boulevard. I walked after school to my first drama workshop. A firmament of dirty stars drifted under my feet. An arch marked the academy's entrance, topped by a wrought-iron sign proclaiming: All the World's a Stage. In Bungalow D, I was greeted by the drama coach, a woman or man, I couldn't be sure. "You can call me B.J." said the coach to a group of gaping adolescents.

B.J. was not only the most masculine, but the most expressive woman I'd ever met. Her baggy shirts and pants rippled after every gesture. She worried a scene into being by plucking her brushy haircut. "Bingo!" she screamed when insight struck.

B.J. ingested a steady stream of Lifesavers and antacid tablets, broadcast directions as a Camel bobbed on the rim of her lips. Once, when she bought a pack of filter-tipped cigarettes by mistake, she took a puff and grimaced. "The draw," she told us, "causes hernia."

B.J.'s choice of scripts was as daring as her jokes. But even with talcum in our hair and crow's-feet painted on the corners of our eyes, the third act of *Death of a Salesman* slogged to an oddly mechanical conclusion. In lieu of Arthur Miller, she proposed we try improvisation. "Actors," said B.J., pointing to a woman at an upright piano, "meet your accompanist, Miss Jean Miller." Jean looked exactly like B.J.—cropped hair, roomy clothes—only one shade paler and more reserved.

We spent an hour on exercises "to stretch the tendons and start the heart." "Be trees," commanded B.J., and we all were trees, or ivy at least, pressed against the walls. "Children, children," B.J. pleaded, "stage center, and I mean pronto." Clumped together in the center of the room, our little forest somehow flourished. Jean was playing "Mountain Greenery." B.J. appraised each gnarl and branch, walking backwards around the room. "What's this?" she asked, cupping her ear, "Do I hear wind?" Writhing up and down the scales, Jean did her best to simulate the flutter and force of a breeze. "Tree in the breeze," B.J. shrieked. "If you see it in your mind, you'll be it."

An elm grew beside the doghouse, the tallest tree in our backyard. During the Santa Ana winds, it shook with such violence and volume, I'd be drawn from my bed and book to the window. Branches heaved in different directions. Leaves quaked on their stems. If I stared long enough, the features of Mother and Father would form in that mass of moonlit motion, their faces fixed for a split second before they shattered and vanished.

That was the tree I pretended to be, and I felt my parents' expressions tremble over my own face, and my body stirred as theirs had stirred—pacing the kitchen or shifting gears—in a search for solace. I was shuddering from confusion too: if opposites made up the world—mother and father, fire and water, past and future—how did my brother's existence fit? Gary was dandled between life and death. And what of B.J., roaming the room, male and female fused in her manner? And what of the present where music resounded, where the bodies of children swayed like trees; did the present lapse into history or lurch into the future?

No amount of algebra could clarify the quandary of time. According to the clocks in our house, time was either slow or fast, but never the same in any two rooms. Or for any two people. The night of the Meglan musical, my father said we were running late, whereas Mother glanced at the kitchen wall clock—a percolating coffee pot—and insisted we had time to spare. She fussed with my cape, bow tie, and top hat.

Martin and Anna arrived at six. My father had me open the door and shake their hands while he filmed us with his camera.

"Should we wave?" Anna asked the lens.

"Just look at Bernard and act surprised."

"Ed," said Mother from the other room, "enough with the camera already."

Anna joined my mother in the kitchen. Martin went to help Gary dress. Father stalked me with the Bell and Howell. "Pretend I'm not even here," he said.

We were gathered at the front door by the time Martin emerged with Gary, who was fully dressed for the first time in months. Martin guided Gary down the hall—brown hands on my brother's shoulders, gold rings glinting in the distance—and together they glided into the light. At that moment, I knew my brother wouldn't live much longer. It wasn't a matter of his bony fingers or the highlights dulled in his downcast eyes; my brother's body had failed him in so many slow, irreversible steps, I'd adapted to every small loss, and I'd dreamed him healthy so often, my dreams overwhelmed his demise. But that Saturday night, in our hall, in our house, my brother was doomed by

Martin's expression, helpless and apologetic. My brother was doomed by my parents' silence; they looked at him and couldn't move. My brother was doomed by Anna's politeness: "Well," she blurted, "everyone ready?"

My three-minute part in the evening's performance was minor, regardless of what B.J. had said about everyone in show business being an important member of one enormous family. I simply bobbed in the background, tipping my top hat on the downbeat as three girls in red leotards kicked their legs to Jean's rendition of "I Get a Kick Out of You." The stage was bordered by footlights, their glow rising like mist. I knew they had to be out there—my parents, my brother, Martin and Anna —and I searched the dark theater for their faces. But each of them remained remote, lost somewhere beyond the light. And when a rumble filled the building, shook the stage, reverberated around the walls, I wasn't sure what caused the applause —pity or pride—and I turned to B.J., wide-eyed in the wings, who flung her hands above her head and shouted, "The house is coming down!"

House Call

B.J. lived with Jean on Wonderland Avenue in Studio City. A caravan of cars left the Meglan Theater and followed B.J.'s orange Volkswagen through the Cahuenga Pass. Mother checked the mimeographed map B.J. had given to the families of the cast while Martin and Anna, their arms around my brother, sang an Arabic folk song, its one hypnotic verse recurring like déjà vu. The façades of apartment houses, row after row set back from the street, were lit by colored lights. Every building bore a name: Tropical Terrace, Charlene Gardens, Paramount Apartments. Some of the newer buildings, walls embedded with glitter, shimmered as we passed.

At the center of the Wonderland Lanai was a swimming pool, empty at that hour, inner tubes and beach balls meandering on its surface. Lit from within, the water flung waves of light on the atrium's four-story walls. The building seemed to rock like a docked boat. B.J.'s door was open on the top landing, her living room—a veritable gallery of movie posters—already crowded with costumed children, parents bragging like press agents, and a collection of B.J.'s theatrical friends, the most animated of her guests, most of whom wore dark sunglasses and turtleneck sweaters. Seconds after we entered, B.J. parted a cluster of people and rushed to us with a six-pack of beer. "Libations?" she asked.

My parents and the Ascerols circled the room, joined in conversations comparing various dance instructors, portfolio photographers, and personnel from the Children's Screen Acting Guild. Gary and I gravitated toward B.J., who was holding court with her friends. "Sincerity is everything in this business," she was saying. "As soon as you can fake that, you've got it made." A black woman with a gold tooth murmured "Shameless" into B.J.'s ear. "Behold," said B.J., yanking me toward her, "one of my flock. Bernard is going to be an actor."

"Architect," I corrected.

"And this is?"

"I'm Gary. Bernard's brother."

"Beautiful eyes. Hasn't he Rodney?" Rodney nodded. "And do you plan to be a star, too?"

"Don't know," said Gary. "But I met a few last summer."

The group went quiet and gazed at Gary. As though testing water, he began by naming a few names, and once he sensed the great degree of interest, dove headlong into description: Tony Curtis's thick eyelashes, Kim Novak's live-in hairdresser, Danny Kaye's taste for garish ties. He told of the children who were subject to every indulgence: a playhouse with hot and cold running taps, a battery-powered Corvette, a sterling silver tea set for dolls. B.J. and her friends were rapt. They interrupted with questions. Their fascination infused my brother. He grew confident, commanding, seemed larger than his frail frame. He claimed the space around him with gestures, his hands drafting extravagant mansions.

Home from B.J.'s, Gary complained of a pain in his chest. Martin and my mother tended him till midnight. I sat with my father and Anna in the living room. To spare me from worry, they spoke in euphemisms, but I knew the *passing*, the *peace*, the *rest* they mentioned was a frightful and final thing. For a year now, all references to death had been banished from the family's conversation, and phrases which had once been common—scared to death, died laughing, dead tired —were carefully avoided. I wasn't sure whether Gary realized he was dying—surely he could have guessed as much from our strained cheerfulness, from the fact that his condition governed our speech and habits—but to ask him would have been unthinkable, and he seemed willing to believe that his burden was merely recuperation. The task at hand, as far as my parents were concerned, was to bolster hope, even if hope entailed deception. They discussed the future in Gary's presence, his return to the water, to the homes of the stars.

As my brother grew gravely ill, my recollection of the boy he had been—black-haired, agile, enterprising—shrunk to the size of a small memento. Sometimes, in the solitude of my room, I'd try to assemble an image of Gary from the vague fragments that floated through my head. That memory might not serve me, that the witnessed bits of my brother's life might not add up to a vivid whole, frightened me more than the probability of his death. Gary would be abandoned to a grave, and forgetfulness fix his absence forever.

In the weeks that followed, Dr. Wertz doubled the dosage of Gary's medication. My parents took turns waking him several times a night, plying him with pills. As a result of one diuretic, my brother was constantly dehydrated; his skin bloomed with scales he scratched and shed. I was seized with panic at the sight of his face and arms. The sour smell of his body was unbearable.

I began to believe, with a new and superstitious conviction, that my brother had become contagious, that remnants of his skin were everywhere, hidden in the carpet or floating on the air, ready to infect me. I kept my door closed. I held my breath in the hall. I would not walk barefoot. I adopted my mother's concern for cleanliness, wiped the doorknobs with disinfectant, ran hot water over forks and spoons. I refused to enter my brother's room, refused to smile with my parents and talk of swimming and college and marriage, even after Martin urged me to be kind.

On a morning early in December, I awoke to the whispers of Dr. Wertz. It was he who phoned the ambulance. I saw Dr. Wertz when I opened my door, the black receiver still in his hand. He stood in the hall and stared at my parents. Side by side, they slumped against the wall. If they moved, I thought, the wall would fall. Time contracted. No one spoke.

The House of God

Aunt Florence, my mother's younger sister, flew in from Chicago for Gary's funeral. The Checker Cab bobbed on its springs as plump Flo, in a floral dress, bloomed out of the back seat. Mother greeted the cab at the curb, nestled her head on Flo's shoulder. "Poor Lilly," Flo said, and let fall her luggage. Entwined together, they wept and petted.

Flo trundled into the house, swamped me in a long embrace, her torso eclipsing my view of the room. "If there's anything you don't understand, ask Aunt Flo." What I didn't understand was why, when my brother's death had been imminent for so long, the actual fact could stun and dispirit my parents and me, as though we never believed it could happen. For a year I had recognized a hundred forms of absence—buildings leveled to vacant lots, decaying leaves swept from the sidewalk, the simple subtraction of cars from the street as our neighborhood went to work—but none served as the slightest preparation. These were routine disappearances, part of the city's thriving life, not at all like someone's death—a private violation. Gary's body is empty, I would say to myself, but still reclining as it had in bed, his eyes locked shut, his heart in hibernation.

Had I possessed the presence of mind to ask my aunt anything, I would have asked why, if no one wants to, everyone dies. Can't science stop it? The six o'clock news was filled with reports of medical miracles: given a strong electrical shock, a dead man's heart began to beat again; a little boy was lifted from a lake and made to breathe by an iron lung. But my brother's body stopped like a watch. No doctor could intervene. No drug helped. No machine reprieved him.

My faith in science crumbled as swiftly as a hotel I'd seen demolished in a newsreel, its supports severed by dynamite, its bricks sinking in a cloud of dust. The books on my bureau, with their utopian claims and idealized drawings, seemed as preposterous, as childish as the comic books they had replaced. And I would have been abandoned to despair had it not been for Flo; her sole duty was endowing cheer. She'd swoop into my room, open her arms, and I'd press against her breast. My aunt was like another planet, its surface cotton and accommodating curves, its atmosphere violet perfume. She'd coddle and rock me, croon songs in a wobbling falsetto: *Que será será, whatever will be will be, the future's not ours to see . . .*

My parents became her wards as well. Father's impatience all but vanished; he sat in the wing chair clutching his knees till Flo sauntered over and shook his shoulders, imploring him to talk. And my father would talk, hesitant at first, staring up into Florence's face, and she'd blot his tears with her handkerchief and chant, "I know, I know." Flo had a harder time with Mother. Mother was mad at God. "Why would God take him?" Mother would ask, tamping the ash from her cigarette.

"Some of us," Flo proposed, "are too sweet for life. And God wants them back."

"Florence . . ." said Mother. And left it at that.

Mother lit the yahrzeit candles, covered the mirror above the mantel. She did the things that God would have wished, but she did them like a grudging girl whose father demands she tend her chores. Often she stopped and listened to the rain, as though its patter contained some message. Finding her sister frozen mid-gesture, eyes narrowed, head cocked, Flo tiptoed up to Mother and whispered, "Lillian? What?"

"Nothing," said Mother. "Nothing is what."

Lester drove us home from the funeral in his black limousine. Drivers who sidled up to us on the freeway tried to peer through the tinted windows, hoping to glimpse a celebrity. Once, Lester was forced to use his horn, the opening notes to "We're in the Money" disrupting my family's reverie. Cora poked him and mouthed "No." Lester looked at Father in the rearview mirror. "Sorry, buddy boy," he said. Father shrugged and leaned against Mother. I had my head in Florence's lap. I reached to turn on the small TV that faced the back seat, but Flo grabbed my wrist and drew it back. "Not right now," she said in my ear, then blew a puff of warm breath.

During the rest of the ride home, I thought about the mortuary, its high ceiling, white walls, the anteroom with its sheer curtain that concealed my parents, my aunt, and myself from the guests who had come to pay their respects. We could see out, but no one could see in. While Rabbi Kaplan delivered the eulogy, the Lavitts and Ascerols glanced at the curtain. This, I had thought, might be like death; one is present and yet unseen; the living look in your direction, and finding no one, turn away. My brother's body lay in its casket, set in satin, surrounded by flowers. He looked small in the distance, blurred by the curtain, a baby in a wooden cradle, Moses floating to rest among the reeds.

As we pulled into the driveway, clouds were breaking apart in the sky. Our house was stained with changing light, the walls turning yellow, lilac, gray. My parents invited the Lavitts in.

Florence collected each of our coats and hung them in the hall closet. My parents' coats were pinned with black ribbons that Florence undid and hid in her purse. Lester stretched, cracked his knuckles, cleared his throat. "Kids," he said to my mother and father, "what can me and Cora do?" Cora had Pudgey curled in her arms; she suggested hot coffee, and maybe later a game of gin rummy. Mother repeated "gin rummy" as though it were a foreign phrase. And then she looked at Cora and laughed. "Yes," said Mother. "Of course."

That afternoon as I made my bed, Florence, who had worn a black dress to the funeral, burst through my door in a pink pantsuit. "Ta-da," she sang, mincing in a circle, arms akimbo. "Hot pink. The latest thing. Whadda ya think?" The pantsuit seemed to generate light, and that, combined with Flo's hennaed hair, caused her to glow like an apparition. "Wow," I said, and swallowed hard. Florence recruited me to help her with a box of Gary's belongings packed by my parents the night before. "Let's not bother your folks with this."

Florence and I crept past the arch that led to the living room. My parents were blowing on cups of hot coffee, their faces flushed from steam. They discussed with the Lavitts how the city had changed.

Father asked, "Where's there cheap land left to buy?"

"There's got to be something," Lester said. "We'll just have to look harder now."

In the ceiling of my parents' walk-in closet was a trap door that opened to the attic. I unhinged the step ladder, held Flo's hand and boosted her up. Each rung creaked as she steadied her feet. She had to pound on the trap door—it hadn't been used in years—and chips of paint snowed on my face. Finally Florence's head and shoulders ascended into the ceiling. "O.K." she called out in a muffled voice, wiggling her stubby fingers for the box. I staggered a moment under its weight and hoisted it into her hands. She grunted and heaved and the box was gone. Some hangers I'd hit were rocking and chiming. The air in the closet was still and close, pungent with mothballs and rose sachet. I waited to help my aunt down, but Florence didn't budge. "Aunt Flo?" I asked, tugging her cuff. "Bernard," she said, "it's weird up here." Then she disappeared.

Afraid to be alone, I hurried after her up the ladder. The attic ran the length of the house, empty except for one box and glowing Flo, who surveyed the space in slow motion. Rolls of insulation padded the roof, a pitch which seemed composed of cloud. A shaft of afternoon light pierced the vent at the far end of the attic and hung rigid in midair. My aunt thrust one hand into the light, her fingers glaring white. She snatched at moving motes of dust. Currents of dust stirred and whirled, sifting in different directions. The distant voices of my parents and the Lavitts wafted up through the floor. The words were unclear but the tone was tender. The rabbi had said that Gary dwelled in God's house. If there was a God, if God had a house, here was his house: a storm of dust in a shaft of light, the soft sound of bodiless talk.

....
CHILDLESS

Make It Good

Yearly, for the past ten years, a friend of mine has told the tale of how she lost her virginity. At first the details were scant and prosaic. A guy named John. An apartment in New York. But my friend discovered embellishment and, endowed with a gift for swift improvisation, she inflated her story out of proportion, an immense balloon improbably bobbing in an annual parade.

Within her rich imagination, John grew like a prize potato, bulbous shoulders, overeager eyes. And his nickname changed year after year. "Joy-boy-John." "Johnny-never-get-enough." "Double-jointed-John-the-love-machine-in-the-edible-jeans." John evolved from friend to neighbor to lascivious sailor, a play where one actor assumes all the parts which escalate with desperate passion. Add to that a dawn in Manhattan, and after it was over, her labored breath in humid air as she counted holes in the soundproof ceiling.

Once you tried to count the stars and only a membrane kept you separate from a new way of life. What is your sexual history anyway except scraps that expand when immersed in memory, like those Japanese flowers composed of pressed paper, blooming silently overnight in a bowl of water beside your bed? No sooner do you think, "So-and-so's kisses were the best," than the mere idea of a kiss ferments, your mouth warm with foreign breath and heady implications. Why shouldn't you lie about one or another of your former lovers, their hidden motives, clever retorts, thrilling techniques. The right exaggeration is a wondrous thing; it's as if you're asleep and the hands of old admirers are falling upon you, light as leaves. And I'm not talking quantity either, though the total recall of a single encounter would mean a commitment to the infinite.

It's almost that time of year again, and I'd like to encourage my friend to abandon her last vestige of reserve. I'd appreciate the introduction of some extravagant angle, some subplot worthy of a Hollywood movie: a pilotless plane or a double agent or a hitchhiking ghost. Look, I want to tell her, there are only so many years left, and there are fewer than one hundred nerve ends in the average finger, and our body's ratio of muscle to fat is shifting like sand in an hourglass. May Johnny's nickname stretch as long as a limousine, its hyphens like the dividing line on a highway to a hedonist's haven. Go on, I want to tell her. Make it good.

The Origin of
Roget's Thesaurus

When Anne-Marie sidles up and bends slightly forward, her
starched uniform crackles like a distant fire, and she discreetly,
yet suggestively, offers potatoes with gravy to Dr. Roget. The
smell of garlic assails his nose, and then the lilac smell of Anne-
Marie, distinct odors fused into something mesmerizing, difficult to name. His nostrils flare. His eyes cloud up. His fork
becomes inconceivably heavy. What precisely is this sensation,
this suffusion of fragrance, appetite, lust? What rubric or term
or adjective could capture it? He thinks *delicious*. No, *delightful*.
Then the panorama of *pleasantness* opens in his brain: *Pleas-
ing, enchanting, appealing,* a vast and verdant country. But further inland, in the dark heart of Dr. Roget's confusion, lies the
antonymous terrain of *unpleasantness,* its odious flora and hor-
rible fauna, and he doesn't know where to turn.

"Peter?" murmurs Mrs. Roget, miles away at the end of the
table.

"Daddy?" murmurs Peter Junior, beneath a branching can-
delabrum.

Hush, hush. Doors are opening in Daddy's head, doors that
lead to halls of doors that lead to other labyrinthine, musty halls
of doors. Door by door, word by word, an entire lexicon will
be discovered. A draft will begin to move through portals, the
wind to whistle fluently, and someday Daddy will reach a door
opening onto the sea.

The moment before we make love, I think about the sea
at night. I'm clutching the sail of your broad warm back.

What tenuous connections, what tributaries of association brought me from the landscape in Roget's brain to your body beyond the limits of land? What convoluted currents of chance, what chain reaction of history took me drifting from my boyhood on the coast of California and propelled me to you, here in this bed in this vessel on the black undulating ocean, to this very second when I can't stop thinking, synapses flashing like stars, the doors in my head opening, opening, the wind of my words against your back: *supple, tractable, bendable, mutable* . . .

Don't Think
About Breathing

You suddenly become aware of the air. Very aware. Carbon and oxygen, ozone and exhaust, steep in the sunlight, tainting the day. Each breeze contains olfactory stimuli, infrared waves, dust motes, pollen, words, and birdsong.

Inhale now. Taste the commotion; rivulets of cool saliva, a brisk wind moving beyond your molars. It's possible that an atom from one of Napoleon Bonaparte's egocentric sighs is grazing your papillae at this very instant. A smattering of microcosmic crumbs from the sum total of human history, with all its plague and war and torture, mingles in your mouth, falls down your glottis. And the ulula dangles at the back of the throat like a tear that will not dry or drop.

Life bombards you with so much suffering, and yet you're enwrapped by ribs. Inside, big vascular bagpipes pump the marching music they play by heart, the only tune they've ever known. Now they're bulbous, full to bursting. Now they sag like withered fruit. Better get used to these vicissitudes. If I were you, I wouldn't think too hard about breathing. Be glad that your lungs, like a pair of auburn bears after winter, revive themselves over and over.

Time and space prevent me from enumerating (and fully understanding) all the complex physiological reactions which result from the pulmonary process. But I know a bit about heavy breathing. I know about the body wracked with passion, the heart seized by speed, the percussion of corpuscles inside the ears, sparks igniting the periphery of vision. I know how fervent the lungs can become hovering above someone and beating, beating, beating like wings.

Duet

As a boy, Lester spent hours with his dummy, whose wooden hair was orange. His hand would get hot in the dummy's head. He made the creaking eyelids blink. He made the mouth move believably. Lester perfected the consonants, forced *m*'s and *b*'s through rigid lips. A voice would gather in Lester's chest, slide up his throat, and fully formed, eagerly conversant, it seemed to come from outside his body, an independent intelligence, tossing off quips as the small tuxedo trembled.

Lester grew older possessing two voices, always at ease with each. Even after Lester lost interest in the dummy, finding its bow tie ridiculous, even after he lay the body to rest, its arms and legs tangled in a box, even after the box was lost, Lester threw his voice and objects talked.

Cora finds him fascinating, a stout enchanted man. When he cooks, pork chops plead for mercy. When he walks, flowers ask to be plucked from their pots. So he consents and presents them to her, bowing low and slyly smiling. The fact that she's cross-eyed doesn't disturb him. He says she just sees two sides to a story.

At sunset, a diamond ring proposes. Since Cora sees two rings her happiness is doubled, innumerable facets catching the light. The newlyweds barrel through the night. Trees along the road sing popular songs. Best wishes issue from windows. The world has a voice, and with it woos Cora. She's never known anything quite like that. Lester concentrates, coughs, breathes. He speaks to the moon and the moons speak back.

Gravitational Attraction

There's a textbook entitled *Human Sexuality* with a painting by Marc Chagall on the cover. It shows a young male and female acrobat. They're balanced on a wire, talking in whispers, costumed in mottled violet and green, arms outstretched toward houses and hills. But wouldn't this make a better cover for a textbook entitled *A Pleasant Friendship?*

During sex I talk a gutteral talk, walk a tightrope taut between speech and babble. The register of my voice goes low. Vibrations escape my shifting ribs. I inhabit every exhalation.

When it's through I'm trapped in a body of lead, crushing innersprings, denting pillows. Exiled from the distant ceiling, I'm purged of things to say. I don't know about you, love, but I feel as huge as a Rodin nude, the bed a disheveled pedestal about to implode from our ponderous torsos.

How about a painting of two lead spheres thrust from Isaac Newton's hands? How about the blur of velocity rising from each like heat? How about a backdrop of houses and hills as faint as a day that is being forgotten?

Everything seems forgotten after sex—money, animals, shoes —everything except that gravity outlasts us, tugs at us in unison, despite our acrobatics. While lying content with my tongue on your neck, I'm aware of gravity, its gradients and magnitude, its horizontal and vertical components, its units of terrible tortion. I know this sensation is nothing new. Even the Greek Ptolemy was bothered by his vague conception of a force tending toward the center of the earth. So were physicists Kepler, Konig, Bailey, Braun, and the myriad objects of their attraction. We are solid volumes sprawled on linen, flattened together, falling in love.

······································

Childless

So I was talking to this guy who's the photo editor of *Scientific American*, and he told me he was having trouble choosing a suitable photograph of coral sperm for an upcoming issue. I was stunned because I'd always thought of coral as inanimate matter, a castle of solidified corpses, though corpses of what I wasn't sure. Of course, I had to find out what coral sperm looks like, and he told me it's round and fuchsia. I could see it perfectly, or so I supposed, as if through an electron microscope, buoyant and livid, pocked like golf balls, floating like dust motes. Still, I couldn't visualize the creature who constitutes female coral, as distinct from male, toward whom one seminal ball went bouncing, like a bouncing ball over lyrics to a song. It was kind of sad to think that, for all its flamboyant fans, osseous reefs, gaudy turrets, coral was one more thing, or species of thing, about which I knew almost nothing, except that it generates sperm, round, fuchsia.

The funny thing about being a man who is childless and intends to stay that way is that you almost never think of yourself as possessing spermatazoa. Semen, yes; but not those discrete entities, tadpoles who frolic in the microcosm of your aging anatomy, future celebrities who enter down a spiral staircase of deoxyribonucleic acid, infinitesimal relay runners who lug your traits, coloration, and surname from points remote and primitive. Certainly you don't believe that the substance you spill when you huff and heave in a warm tantrum of onanism could ever, given a million years and a Petri dish and an infrared lamp, could ever come to resemble you. It would be like applauding wildly at a Broadway play and then worrying that you hurt the mites who inhabit the epidermis of your hands. Death is all around us, and we sometimes assist.

Anyway, there are so many varieties of life, and hardly enough Sunday afternoons to watch all those educational programs that teach you about the reproductive mechanisms of albino mountain goats with antlers that branch off and thin away like thoughts before you fall asleep. And sloths who move so slowly they never dry off from morning dew and so possess emerald coats of mold. And yonic orchids housing pools of perfume in which bees drink and wade and drown.

The first time I was alone in the wilderness, I walked through a field that throbbed with song and wondered whether crickets played their wings or their legs. My footfalls, instead of causing the usual thud, caused spreading pools of solemn silence. Sound stopped wherever I walked. And I walked and walked to hush the world, leaving silence like spoor.

LaVergne, TN USA
09 January 2010
169384LV00003B/34/A